ME AND MY FAMILY AND ME

Stories for Pearl and Everett

By Andrew Dickson

For my family.

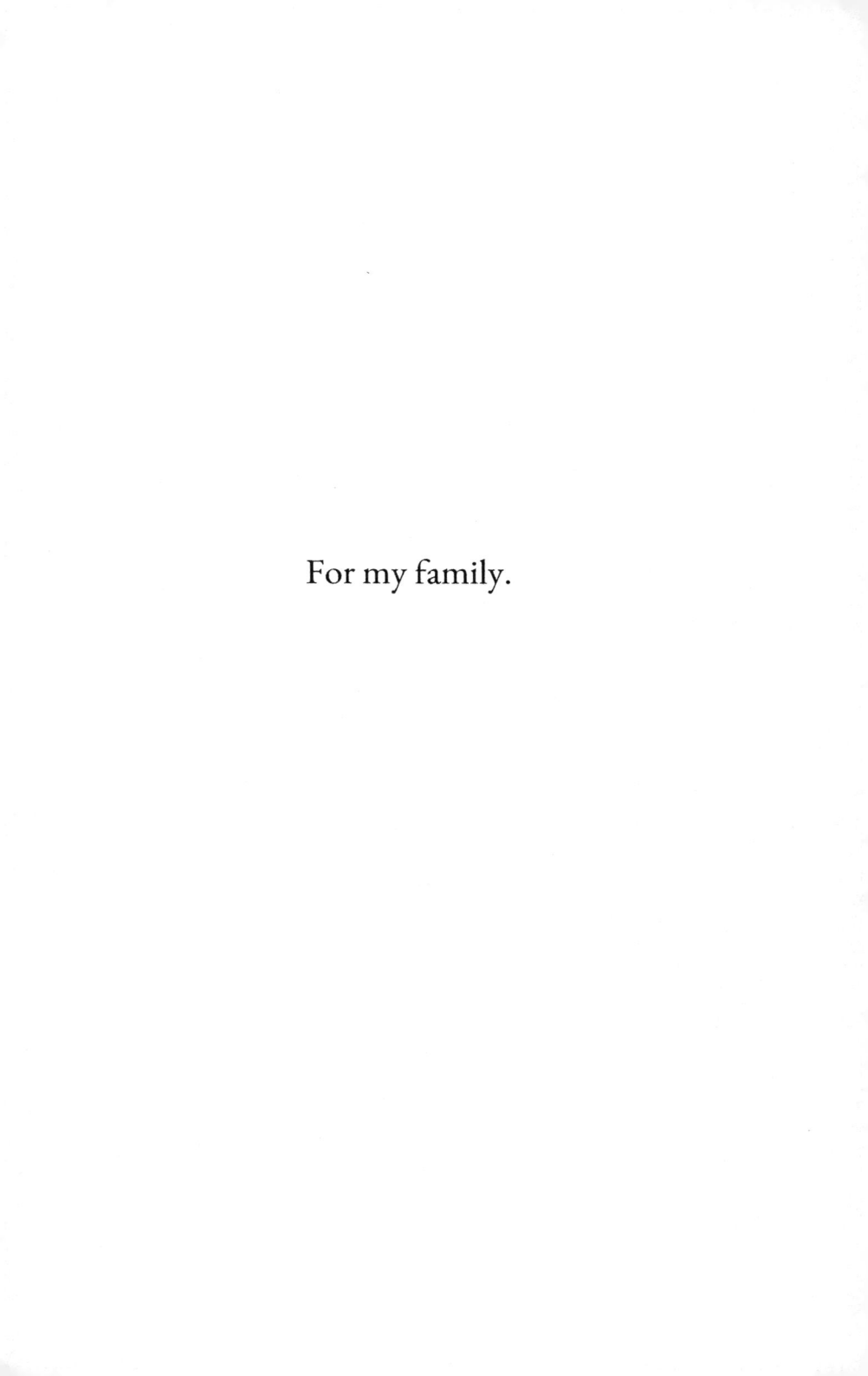

TABLE OF CONTENTS

How This Book Works	5
Candy	8
Monopoly	18
The Navy	25
Church	33
Baseball	45
Baseball Cards	55
Baseball Cards Postscript	62
Lego	66
Game Shows	76
Clubs	85
Books	93
Ice Cream	103
California	110
Ebay	118
Weddings	135
Music	146
Thank You	158

HOW THIS BOOK WORKS

I'm a fan of titles that telegraph what's to come.

As advertised, this is a collection of stories about me and my family. And because I seem best able to remember stories I played a key role in, I added an extra me in the title.

I suspect these stories will be of low interest to strangers, mild interest to acquaintances, but some interest to good friends, and hopefully fascination to my family, who are such a big part of the stories.

I hope my kids, Pearl and Everett, will especially enjoy this collection as they were the inspiration for me to stop telling these stories from time and time and actually write them down.

In fact, I've gone ahead and addressed these stories to them directly.

If you are Pearl or Everett, I hope you will appreciate the gesture and will read this when I give it to you, and then again in a few years. And again and maybe even again some years later.

Everyone else, I trust you can deal with the conceit.

You'll soon notice that these aren't linear beginning, middle, end stories. I tried that at first. But then I hit on this idea of combining a few stories or even just a collection of anecdotes and memories about different family members who share something in common.

So each story is about a thing, expressed by a noun, and incorporates multiple people. I like how the format brings the different parts of my family together, especially when they never had the chance to meet.

Why stories? About a family that has enjoyed, for the most part, a lot of privilege and a lack of tabloid-grabbing drama or gossip?

Well, what else is there that really, really matters other than the stories we have to share?

They can help us understand and learn about experiences we haven't or could never have. And they can help us remember and reflect upon our own.

One of my favorite feelings in the world is hearing a great story and hanging on every word, but at the same time in another part of my mind I'm remembering and reliving something that happened to me.

So while this isn't the whole story, or even all the stories I want to share, I hope it's enough to enjoy and help you remember some of your own stories and memories. Whoever you are.

Let's dig in.

CANDY

You know that huge neon map of America we visit at the Smithsonian Museum of American Art in Washington, DC?

The one by the artist Nam June Paik that you guys love to sit down on the floor and watch - because inside the neon outline of every single state are monitors playing videos about each place.

Some of them are generic, inside of Kansas a scene from the *Wizard of Oz* plays. Others are more personal, like the scenes from a rehearsal for a performance the artist took part in inside Washington State.

I think that's part of what makes the piece so interesting. There's no rule governing the videos, they're based on associations. I think a lot of us relate to places the same way. I know I do.

Vermont makes me think of skiing and snow and that bumper sticker "ilovermont" where the two words slur together, and the first "o" is a heart.

Alaska fills me with longing as it's the only state I've yet to visit, and also the most vast and wild.

Virginia irritates me because the saying goes Virginia is for lovers, Maryland is for crabs. I like crabs, I'm a Cancer after all, but growing up in Maryland I felt like we got the short end of the stick on that one.

And New York fills me with nostalgia and the anticipation of seeing family.

Growing up we went to visit New York four times a year. Twice every summer, again for Thanksgiving, and then again for Christmas. I looked forward to each visit for days beforehand.

Most of my Dad's family lived there. His sister Andi and husband Stephen and their three kids. His brother Peter. And his Mom, your great-grandmother Isabelle, whom we always stayed with. My brother Alex and I called her Grammy Dickson.

Our tips to New York started in the morning, with my parents fitting our suitcases into the minivan like puzzle pieces. We always stopped for lunch in New Jersey at the "fancy" Roy Rogers fast food restaurant.

And by later afternoon we'd drive over the Tappan Zee Bridge in the afternoon crossing impossibly high above the Hudson River and I'd get this feeling of nervous excitement in my chest because we were almost to Grammy Dickson's. I couldn't wait.

You guys would have loved your great-grandmother. She had a huge personality and treasured holding court at the middle of the dining room table surrounded by family. She could hold an entire room's attention, but also knew how to talk to her grandkids without talking down to us or expecting us to act like adults. She would remember details we shared from our last trip and ask questions that would make our imagination work. Like "What would you do with a thousand dollars?" or "What country would you like to live in when you grow up?" Sure beats how's school going? Or even worse, do you have a girlfriend?

Her apartment had a big living room full of art, books and antiques that overlooked the Hudson, but my brother Alex's favorite place was her study. Every visit she'd set up two army cots for us to sleep amongst her towering bookshelves and shelves of inkwells and other small collectibles.

Every night she would come scratch our backs and tell us a story to help us fall asleep. She did this well past the point my brother or I needed tucking in, but didn't we complain. She had long nails, so you could hear them moving against the flannel of our pajama tops. And she spoke in a soft, sing-song voice that made keeping your eyes open almost impossible.

The first night of every visit we would ask her to tell us about the candy store her mom created in her kitchen growing up. It was housed inside a locked pull drawer and filled with rows and stacks and containers full of every kind of candy you could imagine.

Your great-great-grandmother regularly restocked it so it was always as chock-full as a five and dime store case. But she didn't take cash or check. The store only opened for good deeds, better grades and completed chores.

Naturally Grammy Dickson and her siblings spent a good part of their childhood trying to find the key or jimmy the drawer open without it.

Whenever they managed to break in they would each take just a little bit of candy, hoping she wouldn't notice. And they'd eat their stolen candy quickly under their front porch, careful to bury the wrappers a few inches into the dirt.

But your great-great-grandmother always caught them. Parents have a way of knowing when their kids have been up to no good.

It's funny how sometimes we replicate things without even meaning to.

The two of you have a dedicated pull drawer in our kitchen full of snacks. I can see it from where I write this. It's full of snacks like granola bars, microwave popcorn and organic macaroni and cheese and it's not locked, so you guys can open it whenever you want. Every now and then we'll slip some candy in. Especially after holidays when your Grandma Jeanie inevitably gives you full chocolate bars, bags of Hershey kisses and whatever else she was pleased to happen upon as a gift.

And Susan and I loved to tell you guys stories about when we were kids when you were still in need of tucking in.

Everett, for years you had the most amazing bedtime ritual. You'd start by brushing your teeth, then you'd run upstairs and give your worries to our guinea pigs or our puppy Clover. You'd blow air through your cupped hand onto their backs, sometimes even whisper chanting "worries, worries, worries," so they'd all go away.

Then, and only then, were you ready for your bedroom story.

Susan was most often the storyteller. For one, she's great at it. And I am allergic to guinea pigs, having thought I was a mostly allergy-free person until Poppy and Marigold arrived in our house. But a few nights a week I'd find a mask, plentiful since the pandemic, endure the inevitable runny nose, and tell you a story myself.

Usually I'd tell you about my own childhood, or stories from when you were younger. But once, searching my brain for a story you hadn't heard, I told you about your great-grandmother's candy drawer. At first you smiled, but as you thought about having so much candy inside your own house your entire body started to shake and vibrate with excitement.

You both love candy dearly and deeply.

Everett, lollipops were your first love. The first Halloween where you could walk up to a house under your own power, they were all you were interested in. You followed every "Trick or treat!" with "Got any lollipops?"

And if the people giving out candy didn't, which was usually the case, you would about-face empty handed, trot down the stairs and march off to see if the next house did.

I appreciate that you tolerate that story, Everett, but I think it makes you a little melancholy thinking of all the snack-sized Snickers and brown and yellow bags of M&M's you missed out on.

The story you prefer is from Halloween a few years later. The one when Pearl and her friends dressed up as witches and said you could tag along if and only if you dressed as a black cat. So you did.

It was an especially cold and rainy night, so most kids didn't stay out too long. But you two can stand harsh weather in general and even more so when candy is on the line. So you stayed out for hours and hours with Susan and I trailing along behind, ignoring our pleas to come in and get warm. The longer you stayed out the higher the stakes. By night's end, folks were giving out huge fistfuls of candy, lest they be tempted to eat it the next day themselves. So you each came home with an insane haul.

You spent the next hour sorting the different varieties, per usual, creating bar graphs on the carpet to see which types were trending, and trading back and forth. All the while eating as much as we would let you.

Pearl, towards the end of the night, you asked us when the Candy Fairy was coming. "The Candy Fairy?" we asked.

"You know," you explained, "the fairy who comes in the night and takes away all your candy in exchange for a toy."

We had never heard of the Candy Fairy, but seeing a golden cavity-preventing opportunity we thought fast and assured you both she was delayed with so much territory to cover, but would arrive the following night.

So the next day we bought a couple PlayMobil figures and that evening you each eagerly set out your haul for the Candy Fairy before you went to sleep. You awoke to your new toys, happy with the trade.

But what to do with the 14 pounds of candy we now had hidden at the top of our bedroom closet?

I had been doing some auctioneering for nonprofits and schools for a few years by then and had gotten pretty good at it. I was also performing in a variety show where a few friends and I got together once a month in front of an audience. It was called the

New Shit Show because whatever we did had to be new and also because the evening could, if not rehearsed and planned properly, become (if you'll excuse the language) a bit of a shit show.

So for the next performance I came up with the idea of conducting a short auction for my allotted time. Rather than sell anything valuable I grabbed some random things from around the house I didn't need anymore, starting each item off for just a dime or quarter.

I got a few dollars for a t-shirt with a funny logo and a few more for a stack of coffee table books. Then I put that bag of candy up for sale and told the story how the Candy Fairy had enabled me to liberate it from your collective teeth. Two people got in a frantic bidding war and wouldn't you know it, I sold it for $37.

I love that you two love that story. And I think your great-grandmother would too.

MONOPOLY

A lot of people hate the game Monopoly.

Your mom is one of those people. She wonders who could love a game where the purpose is to bankrupt your friends and family. She's got a point.

I tolerate and even at times enjoy it because it reminds me of my mom's Dad, whom my brother and I called Grand Man.

I'm not sure where the idea to call him that came from but it suited him. He was a character, always in a great mood and with a smile that made his eyes twinkle and an arsenal of quips and jokes at the ready.

He was a carpet salesman and later on a carpet inspector. I'm not sure the inspection was a state regulation kind of thing or more of a senior salesman deal. But he was so at ease around people I'm sure he was good at it either way.

We would visit him and my Grammy Hartman in Largo, Florida every spring break, the perfect time to see Spring Training baseball games and enjoy the beaches and bathwater of the warm Gulf of Mexico.

One afternoon was especially hot and we forgot the sunscreen so by the time we were leaving the beach I had one of those sunburns that starts peeling before you're even home. It was pretty bad. To distract me we all played Monopoly that evening.

It took hours. Probably because we weren't getting $500 for landing on Free Parking.

The official rules of Monopoly make it clear that you shouldn't play that way, claiming it makes the game longer. But I disagree. I think infusing extra cash into the game helps people get to the hotel buying stage faster, which is the only way the game ever ends.

Everett, I know you have my back here as ensuring a crisp $500 bill is on the center of the board is something you are insistent and passionate about.

My childhood sunburn game finally came down to my Grand Man and me. We kept playing well past midnight, by far the latest I had ever stayed up, likely because my parents knew the only way I was going to lie on my back and fall asleep was from sheer exhaustion. And it worked. The game took my mind off of my back and when the game was finally over I passed out.

I didn't play a whole lot of Monopoly after that. I was into Dungeons & Dragons and video games. And then just going out with friends.

But Monopoly is one of those games that's always around. In the closet of a beach house rental, or sitting crooked on the game shelf at the Victorian house-turned-coffee shop.

When you two were really young we always went on vacation as a family, all four of us. We still do for the most part but a few years ago I had a revelation. Your mom or I can take just one of you somewhere and it will give us one-on-one time, cost less, and completely eliminate the possibility of the two of you fighting.

Pearl, I feel like the Sou'Wester travel trailer resort up in Long Beach, Washington has become our spot. And I promise we'll work up to San Francisco or New York City soon and maybe even London or Tokyo someday after that.

Everett, you are all about the Kennedy School. The old elementary school turned into a multi-restaurant hotel with a movie theater and a soaking pool right here in Portland.

The first time we went we stayed in an old classroom which was cozier than you might expect. And that sequence of events of that stay created a schedule we've stuck to on subsequent visits. It goes like this.

We check in right at four, throw our stuff in the room, bounce on the bed a few times, then race over to the movie theater, get a good sofa to sit on, buy popcorn *and* candy, run back to our seats and enjoy the afternoon matinee. Then we hit the soaking pool for a long soak, have pizza and burgers for dinner at one of the classrooms turned restaurants, then hit the soaking pool again, read, go to sleep, and then get up, walk over to the nearby grocery store to buy tamales from the vendor outside for breakfast and hit the soaking pool one last time before check out.

If you know a better way to spend 20 hours, I'm all ears.

On one of our early visits we went to the kid-friendly pub for dinner and found a well-loved copy of Monopoly. The kind where the board is hanging together with tape and missing property cards have been recreated with crayon on scraps of paper.

We had so much fun playing that we stopped by a game store on the way home the next morning and bought our own copy.

These days there are dozens of versions of Monopoly, mostly themed around movies and tv-shows. We chose one of the many Star Wars versions, specifically the 40th Anniversary Edition, which highlights the original film I call *Star Wars* but you guys call *New Hope* or just *Number Four*.

It's similar to regular Monopoly but instead of landing on Virginia Avenue you land on "Jedi Mind Trick" which features an image of Obi-Wan Kenobi.

But the rules, board layout, property prices and rents are the same as the original game.

We got home, opened it up and played it that very afternoon. One whole game starts to finish. And then we played another game the next day and another the day after that. We played that game every single day for two months straight. One entire start-to-finish game of Monopoly every single day and sometimes, if we were really feeling it, we'd play twice.

People marvel at the feat. How did we make the time?

Well, turns out the game goes pretty quick when it's just two people. Especially when one of them is a motivated 8-year old who rolls and moves the tokens for both players and memorizes the rents for landing on every single property with every number of houses and of course a hotel. Or in our case star fleets or a base.

But the real trick is paying $500 when you land on Free Parking. That way when someone does have a monopoly, they have enough cash to start building and charging more money immediately. It speeds up the game to the point where Everett and I could start and finish a full game inside of an hour.

Everett, no matter how busy you get, or what you get into. I hope you'll always have time to play the occasional game of Monopoly with me.

THE NAVY

There is a bridge alongside the New Jersey turnpike where your Great-Grandfather, aka my Grand Man, was in the Navy.

Whenever we drove over it, my parents would ask my brother Alex and me where we were, and before we could answer they would harmonize "where Grand Man was in the Navy" like the chorus of an otherwise unwritten show tune.

Years later I realize I don't completely understand. Was he stationed on a base or ship nearby? Or did he actually serve on the bridge itself? And if so, why did a bridge in Delaware need Navy protection? I'm going with he was stationed nearby.

My dad was in the Navy too. After he graduated from college he moved to Sweden for a year, and then spent a few months hitchhiking around Europe. While he was traveling his draft notice for the Army came in the mail. This was when the invasion of Vietnam was still being called a "conflict" and getting out of the draft was possible for college graduates with white-collar commitments.

His parents had no idea how to reach him, so by the time my Dad got home he had to enlist. The local draft board told him the only way to get out of the Army call-up was to apply for the Navy. So he did.

He spent most of his three years on an aircraft carrier, and later entertained my brother and I with stories of living on a ship so big it sounded like a city. It had several barbershops, and was so big that when the future Dallas Cowboys star quarterback Roger Staubach spent a summer on the ship they held full scrimmages on deck without anyone getting anywhere near the edge of the ship or the airplanes taking off and landing.

My dad started writing in the Navy selling his first article to the New York Times. And then when his service was up, he took advantage of a deal the Navy had where they would drop you off anywhere in the world and come back a year later and take you home. He chose Spain, and continued pitching and writing articles to magazines which is how he started his career as a writer.

I knew from a pretty young age I would never join the Navy or another branch of the military.

Partly it was growing up in Garrett Park, Maryland, the small town in the DC suburbs I grew up in where you two have gotten to visit dozens of times.

When I was a kid it was home to a lot of aging lefties and radicals.

When I was really young my parents would take me to visit their friends the Reynoldses, who were hardcore liberals. They would let me play with old toy cars on the floor of their screened-in porch while they made cocktails and talked politics with my parents.

When I got a little older I got a gig mowing the lawn for another older couple, the McLaughlins. They were socialists as were many of their friends. The husband, Donal, had been an architect in the Office of Strategic Services during the war. He was tasked with designing the courtroom for the Nuremberg Trials in order to make the Nazi defendants look as guilty as possible when they took the stand. He also designed the U.N. logo.

Probably on account of all these lefties and socialists, Garrett Park was the first place in America to declare itself a Nuclear-Free Zone, which garnered quite a bit of press. Nearby Takoma Park, Maryland and then Berkeley, California soon followed suit with their own declarations.

If you're wondering what exactly a Nuclear Free Zone is, it means it's illegal to transport nuclear weapons through the area.

Garrett Park is no more than a mile square and comprises maybe 250 houses. So when the ordinance or bylaw or whatever was passed when I was a kid, I thought it was kind of silly. The only street through town wasn't big enough for a truck carrying a nuclear warhead to drive on. And if the government figured out how to make it work, who was going to stop them? Not the Reynoldses or McLaughlins. They were in their 80s.

But that wasn't the point.

It was more of a statement. One that helped impress upon me that war was wrong and that there were ways to stand up against it.

By the time I was a teenager, war movies and TV shows had evolved from chest-thumping affirmations of American dominance to gory testaments to the insanity and brutality of armed conflict. So aside from the anti-war way in which myself and your mom were both raised, we had also seen over and over again what awaited us if we served.

Growing up in DC, it was easy for me to see the ravages of war. I visited the Vietnam Memorial as a kid, and seeing walls and walls of names of soldiers killed, many of the teenagers, was powerful and sobering.

Driving through the city, we saw veterans living on the streets still suffering. You didn't have to guess if they had served in Vietnam. All too often their sign for help said so, or they still wore part of their uniform.

And I had friends growing up whose families had immigrated to escape the horrors our country had inflicted across Southeast Asia.

So by the time I was in high school I wore a peace sign necklace without irony and regularly went to anti-war rallies. When my friend Nick started an Amnesty International chapter at our school, I was there at every meeting, writing letters, listening and learning.

During my junior year the US invaded Iraq for the first time. My friend Brad's mom started calling me and advising me on different ways to get out of the draft. She had helped friends avoid the draft during Vietnam and was eager to share what she learned with her son's friends. I suspected that if there was a draft my privilege would prevent me from getting drafted, but I took her calls and listened every time.

Around this time one of the guidance counselors at my high school organized an assembly that was essentially a pro-war rally complete with the school band playing patriotic songs while we were expected to stand with our hands on our hearts.

I was livid. I was sitting next to Nick and whispered we should stand up and march out. He calmed me down, saying "Now is not the time." So we sat there, not standing, but not saying anything either. He wasn't wrong to say what he did, but I was wrong to listen. I regret not standing up, shouting "this is bullshit," and walking out.

I wonder what kind of person I would have become if I had stood up during that assembly. More political? Even less conflict-averse had I been punished in some way? More willing to stand up and act when what's wrong is right in front of me?

Pearl, I know you wouldn't have hesitated to stand up all by yourself for what you believe. One silver lining of distance learning during the pandemic was hearing you engage with your teachers and take the lead on so many of your classroom discussions about anti-racism, why Black Lives Matter, and advocating for the rights of trans people.

Everett, you're not quite as stand up in front of a classroom full of people and say something as your sister. But I know your heart and beliefs are in the right place. Some of my favorite memories of the pandemic are of taking long walks with you and for the first time really talking about politics, history, and systemic racism of our country and the horrific violence against

Black people at the hands of police. You eagerly took me up on the invitation to go on walks day after day.

It's hard for me to imagine either of you wanting to join the Navy, or any branch of the armed service. You are both much more likely to join the anti-war movement. And I hope that never changes.

CHURCH

I was raised freelance.

It was as close to religion as your Uncle Alex and I had growing up.

My parents identified as self-employed more than anything else, and a lot of the lessons they taught us were rooted in working for themselves.

As a belief system, it's a pretty good one. Work hard, but work for yourself. Try and choose projects you're excited about so you'll do your best work.

And when you're not working do something fun. Like going on vacation.

My parents had grown up Catholic and Protestant. But by the time I was old enough to ask them if there was a God they made eye contact with each other for a moment before explaining they didn't necessarily believe or not believe in God. They just didn't *need* him.

They told us we were agnostic. Or at least they were. Not the answer I was expecting as church was everywhere when I was growing. This was the era of celebrity televangelists who used their platform to condemn homosexuality and assure viewers God himself wants us all to call the 1-800 number flashing at the bottom of the screen and hand over our life savings.

That one conversation was kind of the extent of my religious upbringing.* We weren't atheists, or anti-religion. We just didn't talk about it unless I brought it up.

I was curious. Most of my friends were Catholic so they all went to church every Sunday and even went on overnight retreats which sounded super fun. So every now and then I'd ask my parents if we could go to church sometime and they always said sure, but we never went. Kind of how I will on occasion say "sure" to something you guys want to do that I don't.

One year my friends recruited me to play on their church basketball team. This was the era of the big man, when every team needed a Kareem or Patrick Ewing. I wasn't very good, but I was tall.

So I joined the team and was having fun until the practice when the high-school-aged coaches asked me to stick around for a minute. They asked me if I had been baptized.

I had no idea what that meant. After registering my confused expression they told me I couldn't be on the team anymore. And I watched the first game from the stands.

So that left a sour taste in my mouth as far as organized religion goes.

I stopped asking about going to church after that and didn't really think about going until my 21st birthday, which I spent in Cannes, France, visiting my mom's cousin Betsy.

Betsy was a lawyer, the very first American woman to pass the French bar exam which is based on the Byzantine Napoleonic code. She also had an open invitation for relatives to come stay in the apartment on the top floor of her house.

I had planned to spend my birthday there with my friend Bill Tsitsos, who was spending his junior year of college in Greece. But he learned if he stayed for six months he would become eligible for the compulsory Greek military draft, because his Dad was still a citizen. That was not something Bill was interested in (for reasons discussed in *The Navy* chapter), so he went home to Albany before I arrived in France. And so I stayed at Betsy's apartment by myself.

The morning of my birthday she took me to church because it was a Sunday and that's what she did. The service was in French, which I don't speak, so I didn't understand any of it. But between the singing and the ancient high-ceilinged church it was a moving experience. If not spiritually, at least aesthetically.

After the service we went to the harbor and took a ferry over to a nearby island with a group of other well-intentioned local citizens to spend the day picking up trash. I was leaning over to grab a potato chip wrapper when Betsy tapped me on the shoulder, made the international sign to be quiet, and waved me back to the ferry.

We took it right back to Cannes, leaving everyone else to do the clean up. Then we had lunch with the Mayor. They spoke French so I didn't understand much, but the food and marina views were quite nice.

That night, she set out a dinner of cheese, bread and wine and we finally talked in English, catching up on family and my plans for the future. Kind of a strange 21st birthday, but a memorable one.

Betsy died a few years ago but she had a storied life and career, ending with her appointment to the American Counsel in Cannes, a great honor with diplomatic responsibilities.

Despite that experience I continued to think of church as an institution designed to make a few people feel safe and welcome and at the expense of everyone who looks and believes differently.

And there are plenty of churches that operate that way. Preaching one thing and practicing another. Or worse, preaching things that don't align with what

Jesus or Allah or whoever they worship stood for and believed.

I always knew intellectually there were good and even great churches out there, ones that were truly welcoming to all and making differences in not just the lives of their congregation but their entire communities.

But I didn't experience a church like that until your Grandma Jeanie moved here to Portland to live in the apartment we had built for her above our garage.

As you both know, church is hugely important for Jeanie. She's a lifelong Episcopalian who has made some of her closest friends through church, and credits her faith for keeping her alive through several battles with cancer. Leaving her church in Raleigh, North Carolina was one of her biggest concerns about moving West to live next door to us.

Luckily she found a wonderful new community at St. David's which is a short walk from our house here in Portland. It's the kind of place where everyone really is welcome, and the priest is a woman with dyed green hair. It's a neighborhood space too, as you know all too well Pearl, having attended theater camp in their community space ever since you were little.

Almost immediately Jeanie made a host of new friends there, many of whom similarly moved here later in life to be closer to their kids and grandkids, like her best friend Sabine.

I've gone to service there a few times, but I have yet to feel fully comfortable despite how warm and welcoming it is. But I was able to see the power of a church community up close when Betty Jo and David started coming there, first to sell their Street Roots newspaper to the congregation, and then to also attend the Sunday service.

You remember Betty Jo's big huge loving personality, but you might not remember she is a mom and a grandmother and had a career as a hospice nurse. You likely remember David leaning in to hear you due to his hearing, but maybe not that he's an avid reader and political junkie, was a short order cook for decades and was later one of the leaders of Dignity Village, the vital and visible houseless community that persisted for years downtown before civic "progress" enveloped it.

Betty Jo and David met and fell in love while they were houseless, living on the streets.

A few months after they joined the St. David's community, your mom and I made plans for the four of us to travel East to see family for the holidays. We planned to come back to Portland the day after Christmas.

Knowing that Betty Jo and David were spending the holidays in their tent, and not wanting to be all alone for her favorite holiday, Jeanie invited them to come spend the night Christmas Eve.

I'll be honest, we were a little wary. We hadn't met Betty Jo and David yet and we were going to be all the way across the country. But we had nothing to worry about.

The three of them had a wonderful time, especially as David is an excellent cook and Betty Jo is a talker like Jeanie. After some hot showers, home cooked meals and some overdue and much enjoyed TV watching,

Betty Jo and David went home Christmas night. We heard all about it the next evening and were so pleased.

A few weeks later Betty Jo and David's camp got swept, which is another way of saying the cops came by and told everyone that they had to take down their tent, pack up their worldly possessions and leave. No matter that no one had anywhere to go, or any way to get there or even the means to move everything they owned.

When Grandma Jeanie heard through the church grapevine she set into action, getting Sabine to drive to their camp and load them and their possessions into her minivan. She explained the Lord spoke to her and said, "invite them in."

And so she did.

They moved in for six months. Long enough for Jeanie and a few of her friends from the church to really rally around Betty Jo and David and slowly but surely get them back on their feet.

I would be lying if I told you it was easy. I'm not sure how much you two sensed that or not. You were a little younger and it was, in many ways, fun and exciting to have two more people living inside our compound.

You guys would go next door every weekend for movie night, crowding on the couch with Betty Jo and Jeanie while David set his chair right next to the TV so he could hear.

Once the weather warmed up, Susan and I would sit by the open window in our kitchen and listen to you guys all laughing louder than the movie, Betty Jo's laugh loudest of all. It was always a kid's movie, you guys being kids, but that suited everyone fine. Movies had been far and few between for Betty Jo and David.

But there were also challenges. Jeanie gave them her own bed for the first month of their stay and slept on the couch before that became unsustainable. After a while, she got her bedroom back but it was still a lot to have three people living in a one-bedroom apartment. Especially when two of them are suffering from the trauma of being houseless for so long.

They gave us a valuable education as to how difficult that truly is.

Do you remember the day Betty Jo came home from the eye doctor? She looked at us through her new eyeglasses and said she finally knew what we all looked like. For years she couldn't see anything in focus.

But even in casual conversation we got to know firsthand the challenges of living without running water, electricity, or basic human respect from others.

Eventually Betty Jo was able to find a full-time job, and David got help applying for and qualified for disability, so they were able to move into a small apartment. They went from houseless to having a place to call their own, with a door that locked and a shower and sink that worked and lights and a stove and a TV with Netflix, and all that stuff we take for granted.

It happened because Betty Jo and David wanted it to happen and did the long hard work it took.

It also happened because Jeanie and her friends and the church, but especially Jeanie, were with them every step of the way. They rallied together to put the time in to navigate the system and advocate for Betty Jo and David.

Several years later they are still there, in their apartment. There are still challenges. But they are housed and happy. And it wouldn't have happened without Jeanie's faith and her acting on it.

She believes in the power of prayer. And boy does it work for her. I envy her faith. But I have my own beliefs.

I believe in the power of unconditional love and selfless action. That's what Jeanie offered and was a catalyst of change for Betty Jo and David.

I hope that's what you get from your Grandma Jeanie. It's not enough to want or wish or pray for something to change or better.

You have to roll up your sleeves, or in her case give up her bed, and make it happen.

*The only time I ever set foot inside a church as a kid was to see my cousins in the Christmas Pageant when we visited them around the holidays. I mostly remember straining to pick them out up there on stage beneath all those wigs and flowing robes. "Is that Amanda?" "I'm not sure. That might be Chris. Or maybe that's him over there?"

BASEBALL

Your grandpa Paul grew up going to see the New York Yankees with his uncle George, who also served in the Navy during WWII. This was during one of the team's many golden eras, when they had players like Joe DiMaggio, Yogi Berra and Phil Rizzuto.

Your uncle Alex and I grew up going to see the Baltimore Orioles. It wasn't exactly a golden era for them, but we did enjoy one golden year when we were kids.

But even before seeing baseball I knew I wanted to play it, so I got my parents to enroll me in t-ball. The version of the game where you hit the ball off a plastic tube instead of having a pitcher throw the ball your way.

My very first at-bat I confidently walked to the plate, took a swing and sent the ball hurtling towards the outfield. And then I stood there. I had no idea what to do next.

I doubled down on the rules soon after and tried to learn as much about the major leagues as I could. I started following pro baseball and every morning I'd run out to our driveway first thing, grab the Washington Post, pull the sports page out from inside the rest of the paper to pore over the box scores as I ate breakfast.

I would read up on every game, but I would study the Orioles results like a treasure map. Especially if I had listened to the game on the radio the night before.

Some sports are too fast to imagine or even follow when they are only described but baseball is perfect. Most of the time it's a showdown between the pitcher and hitter, and there are so many balls, strikes, and pauses for walks to the mound that the radio announcers have the time and space to create their own style and form a relationship with their audience. A good baseball radio broadcast will draw you in so you're paying even more attention than if you could see it because you're imagining it.

These days folks who grow up as close to DC as I did can root for the Nationals. But my childhood was during the many decades after the Senators had left, and before the Nats arrived. So our family allegiance was to the north of us up in Baltimore. They were the closest team to us geographically, but also where my mom's family was from. Her parents, grandparents and even great-grandparents were all from there, and she was born in nearby Catonsville.

Grammy and Grand Man had retired to Florida by then, which only served to make our collective love of the game stronger, as we visited every spring break when Spring Training was in full swing.

My grandparents lived in Largo, near Tampa and very close to Clearwater where the Philadelphia Phillies played their Spring Training games. Alex and I loved going because it almost felt like going to a high school game. The stadiums were tiny, and the crowds were small so you could get great seats right by the field for cheap. And the players were coming off their off-season so they were in a good mood, usually more than happy to come over to autograph our program.

My Dad had loved baseball as a kid and fell in love with the game all over again with Alex and me, so much so he started writing books about baseball. So for him Spring Training was a chance to catch a few games, but also talk to managers and coaches and other sports writers about whichever baseball book project he was working on.

Our Spring Break trips went on hiatus when Grammy moved back to Baltimore for a few years. My Grand Man didn't come, he stayed in Florida. My mom explained to Alex and I that they had some problems to work out in their marriage. I appreciated and still appreciate her honesty.

My mom is the one everyone can count on. She's always kept in close contact with her family, tries to help mediate disagreements, and is the one relatives know they can turn to when they need help. She's a born problem-solver.

So while my Grammy was moving home where she still had roots, I think having my mom just down the road was also a big reason.

Baltimore is an hour's drive from Washington DC but feels like a world away.

DC is an open book and will gladly point out its key attractions. It's a national, if not international, city. Most people aren't from there and if there is an accent, it's the sound of people enunciating so clearly that where they came from can no longer be heard.

Baltimore is more aloof and less likely to roll out the red carpet. The Inner Harbor is very touristy, but feels intentionally designed to insulate the rest of the city from visitors. And there is decidedly a Baltimore accent, where a's become o's. Maybe because of the O's, aka the Orioles?

I loved it when Grammy came to visit us. But I loved it even more when we went to visit her, because it usually meant we'd go see an Orioles game too.

When I was a kid, they played in Memorial Stadium in the heart of the city. To avoid traffic, my parents would park for free a dozen blocks away and we'd walk through neighborhoods that came alive on game day to get to the stadium.

Every house with a yard would let you park on it, with the prices rising from three to five to ten dollars as you got closer. There were ticket scalpers, teenage popcorn vendors, and adults selling unofficial t-shirts, felt pennants and programs as Orioles fans marched together towards the stadium.

My favorite player was Eddie Murray, a home run hitter who was so beloved the entire crowd would chant "Eddie, Eddie" every time he came to the plate. He was one of those players who hits well in the clutch, far more likely to hit a home run late in a close game with runners on base than when it wouldn't mean as much.

I also liked Jim Palmer. He was their star pitcher in the 1970s, but by the time I was following the team he was in the twilight of his career. He was also an underwear model so you'd be reading a magazine and turn the page and there he'd be, in a black and white photo sitting on a stool staring you down only wearing a pair of jockey shorts, or "tighty-whities" as we called them.

One year we planned to go see a game for my birthday and he was scheduled to pitch. Grammy Hartman ran into him at a supermarket the day before and explained her grandson was coming to see him pitch on my birthday. He signed an autograph and promised a win. And sure enough, he had a game that reminded folks of his glory days, and the Orioles won.

Part of me wonders if it really happened. What are the chances Grammy and Jim Palmer shopped at the same grocery store? But then again back in those days there were no Whole Foods or even Trader Joe's, and star athletes didn't have personal assistants who did all their errands for them.

And Grammy wasn't one to invent things.

In 1983 Eddie and Jim were joined by the rookie Cal Ripken who was good from the get go. So they had star power but also a great supporting cast.

Players like Rick Dempsey, a mediocre hitter, but a good catcher and a great entertainer. In baseball when it rains they delay the game, hoping the sun comes back out. The ground crew would come out and cover the infield with a huge green tarp, so the dirt didn't turn to mud. And you have to just sit there getting wet and hope the rain stopped soon enough for the game to resume.

That's when Rick Dempsey would emerge from the dugout wearing his leg pads and pantomime an entire game all by himself. He'd run to the pitcher's mound, throw an imaginary ball, and then run to home plate and pretend to hit it, dramatically watching it sail over the fence before running the bases. As he rounded third and had a good running start he'd fall to his knees and slide on his pads all the way to home plate. It was almost as much fun as an Eddie Murray game-winning grand slam.

1983 was the year to root for the Orioles. They won their division, facing the Chicago White Sox for a chance to go to the World Series. We scored tickets to game 2, a weekday game, and my Dad proudly wrote a note to my teacher explaining exactly why I would be missing school that day.

They lost that game but won the series and went on to win the World Series against our Spring Training friends the Philadelphia Phillies. Cal Ripken Jr. won Rookie of the Year and if you were me and my brother or any other Orioles fan, you would have thought it was the start of something incredible. But it was downhill from there.

Jim Palmer retired after that 1983 series. In fact his last appearance was a win during that championship run. Eddie Murray was traded a few years later. And the Orioles haven't returned to the World Series since.

Cal Ripken went on to play in every single game for the next decade and half, a huge baseball record that will probably stand for decades. And keep in mind the baseball season is long. Over one hundred and sixty games a year. I wonder how much it bothered him that the Orioles' best season was his very first. Probably a lot. Kind of how Orson Wells made *Citizen Kane* when he was in his early 20s and spent the rest of his career trying to get unfinished projects financed.

When I was in high school Grammy Hartman moved back to Florida to be with Grand Man again.

And Memorial Stadium was replaced by Camden Yards, the first of the new generation of stadiums with fancy food and more luxury everything. It also had a "retro" feel, with stepper risers so the fans were closer to the action and a fantastic view of the Baltimore skyline. It was just off the highway on the DC side of the city for easy access and had more than enough parking.

But for me it never held quite the Baltimore magic that Memorial Stadium had over the decades.

BASEBALL CARDS

The 1952 Mickey Mantle rookie card is one of the most iconic and valuable baseball cards ever printed. One recently sold for 12 million dollars.

When they were teenagers, my dad and my Uncle Peter had two of them.

Old baseball cards are valuable because lots of collectors want them and yet very few of them are still around in good condition. Kids used to play with cards like toys, throwing them like darts or putting their favorites in their bicycle tire spokes until they got wet and fell apart. Entire collections were tossed in the trash when kids got older and outgrew them.

Everyone held onto their stacks of National Geographic magazines instead, thinking they were going to be worth a fortune, which is why they are all worthless. All supply, no demand.

Your grandfather Paul and great-uncle Peter knew baseball cards were worth holding onto so they would go door to door asking folks if they had any old baseball cards they wanted to give away. A lot of folks did so they amassed a vast collection.

When my Dad was away to college, my grandparents moved to a new house and during the move they all went missing. The cards were packed into fancy felt-covered boxes meant for storing silver and fine china, and they never made it to the new house.

The theory has always been that the movers took the boxes thinking they were getting silverware, and were so mad they got baseball cards instead they threw them out.

But I wonder if they didn't peek inside, see all those cards and decide to steal them anyway. Even if they weren't aware of their value, the movers might have just been baseball fans. This was Yonkers, New York after all. Yankees country.

So when my brother Alex and I fell in love with baseball and started amassing baseball cards, we started our collections from scratch. But we built them quickly, spending all our allowance and lawn-mowing money on cards.

Our parents would take us to the baseball card store regularly. The House of Cards in Wheaton, Maryland was our favorite.

It was just a store in a strip mall, with big picture windows filled with faded baseball cards paper-clipped to floor to ceiling blinds, so the name was technically accurate. Inside it was cramped and devoid of natural sunlight. But we thought it was paradise. It felt like every single baseball card that ever existed was inside that store.

We also went to baseball card conventions, where dealers from around the area would fill the room with tables covered with boxes and binders of their best cards.

To bring in more collectors, the organizers would often hire professional baseball players to sign autographs for a few hours, many of whom neglected to pay taxes on the money, which would cause trouble for a few of them with the IRS.

I was so taken by these conventions I held one on my porch. I charged friends a few dollars to set up their "booth" and put flyers around the neighborhood encouraging other kids to come. And kids actually came.

My Dad enjoyed seeing our collections grow, and he was especially excited when a friend of his offered us an entire childhood card collection.

It was boxes and boxes of cards, mostly from the early 1970s, a full decade before my brother and I started collecting in 1981, back when legends like Hank Aaron and Wille Mays were still playing. So we were beyond excited.

My dad and Uncle shared their baseball card collection. But Alex and I kept ours separate.

So to divide this grand gift we held a draft, taking turns picking individual cards and then moving onto entire boxes once we worked our way through the star players.

The biggest prize was a Mike Schmidt rookie card. He played for the Phillies, the team the Orioles beat in their lone World Series victory of our childhood. But he was a three time MVP and his first card was already worth a few hundred dollars, a fortune to us both at the time.

There were two of them in this collection, one in good condition, the other one not so much. Being older I managed to argue my way into the first pick and took the better one. So perhaps it's time I pass mine along to Alex.

Especially as I haven't so much as glanced at my collection since I was in high school and neither of you seem particularly interested in them.

I'm not exactly sure how baseball cards took up so many hours and weeks and years of life. When my Dad was a kid he would play games with their cards, tossing them like throwing stars to see who could get closest to the wall.

I didn't play games with them or even read the statistics on the back of the cards. How did I manage to spend so much time poring over them?

A clue is in how you guys play with the things you collect.

Everett, you have had a long on-again, off-again love affair with Pokemon cards. And while you will on occasion play the game they are designed for, what you love most is to sort your cards.

Sometimes you'll divide them by type, or by their most powerful attack. You even went through a sorting-them-alphabetically phase. You put your best cards in plastic sleeves inside your binder, and you love to trade them with friends. I love watching when you get a really good new card, and have to take half of your cards out and rearrange them to make room for the new one.

Pearl you have mostly moved on from toys, but you had American Girl Doll, Playmobil and Japanese eraser phases, to name just a few. And you know what you did as much if not more than play with your American Girl doll Molly, or other toys? Pore over the catalogs that come in the mail every few months, choosing a favorite thing on each page, and make long lists of all the accessories and sets you hoped to one day acquire.

I recognize all of these behaviors because they are what I did with my baseball cards. Sort and sort and re-sort them. Trade them back and forth with friends. And fantasize about all the great cards I was saving up to get one day as I leafed through baseball card price guides and monthly magazines.

BASEBALL CARDS POSTSCRIPT

In college I fell in love with filmmaking and moved out to Portland largely inspired by the movies Gus Van Sant was making here.

Right out of the gate I made a feature film called Good Grief. It was about a group of kids based on the Peanuts characters who are into Dungeons & Dragons and go on a road trip looking for buried treasure. I shot it on real 16mm film and it took many years to make, and more than all of my money. And while it didn't win or even get into Sundance, I had a blast making it and took it on tour for two months, screening it at movie theaters, record stores and punk rock house basements.

When I got home I wanted to keep making movies, but I had to get pretty resourceful and make short videos on the cheap.

My first short video was inspired by baseball cards.

When I was a kid the dealers seemed like the most successful adults I knew. After all, they had 100 times the baseball cards my brother and I owned together.

As I grew older I saw them differently, often barely making it at one end of a strip mall. Some of them didn't even seem to like customers, kids especially, and they were often more interested in making money than baseball.

I had worked as a production assistant on a film shoot out at the sprawling Nike corporate campus just outside Portland and marveled at the reserved parkings space for all their sponsored athletes.

Michael Jordan had his own parking space, which I guess made sense. But so did Rollie Fingers, a pitcher who was not exactly a household name and had retired a decade before. It seemed absurd to give him his own designated spot on the off chance he came to visit.

I got to thinking how a baseball card dealer specializing in autographs might think to hang out around these spaces and catch athletes unawares.

I cast my friend Bill Bailey as Mark Swanson, dubbing him CEO and lone paid employee of the fiction online business Autographhss.com - the joke being he couldn't get his desired domain name so added an extra h and s.

I asked my friend Steve MacDougall to come film what I imagined would be Bill walking around the campus trying and failing to find any athletes. That was about as thought out as my idea was. I spent more time driving around to third stores with Bill finding garish pastel sweatsuits for his wardrobe than developing a plot or even a script.

A few days before the shoot day I was playing pick-up basketball and sprained my ankle so bad I needed crutches. The visual of me on crutches was too good to pass up, so I cast myself as Kenny, Mark Swanson's unpaid and subservient "VIP in training."

And good thing, because instead of Bill just wandering around not finding athletes his character started unloading on mine about their shared lack of success. There was suddenly some conflict, which is one of those crucial ingredients needed for drama and a good story.

Just when we weren't sure how to end the film, a security guard wandered over and asked us what we were doing. He very patiently waited as Bill's character introduced our company and our hope to find some athletes to get some "autographhss", all while Steve filmed, before politely asking us to leave. It was the perfect ending.

We went home and a few days later had a little video that strangely opened all the doors the feature film I had spent years on hadn't. We got into film festivals, a dot com company hired us to help land ESPN as a client, and the Northwest Film Festival let us host opening night in character. Best of all, I realized I loved performing.

LEGO

I held onto every single baseball card and comic book I ever collected thinking one day my kids will love these. So far not so much.

Good things I held onto my Lego too.

Pearl, you have a deep love for Lego. And Everett, the best way I can describe your synchronicity with Lego bricks and most especially the small people or "mini-figs" is that it's a language you speak fluently.

Both of your introductions to Lego came during a stressful few days when you were just five and three respectively.

Susan had noticed a swollen place on your neck, Pearl, and took you to see the pediatrician. The doctor drew a circle around it with a black sharpie and said if it grows bigger than the circle, go to the emergency room.

It kept growing, so we all four went to the children's hospital that evening.

Knowing the wait might be long and that Everett, you'd need something to do, we grabbed a Lego "Mystery Minifigure" along with various other must-haves from the drugstore on the drive over.

The mini-figure came inside a foil packet where one of 16 different unassembled figures, ranging from athletes to knights to monsters, all with lots of accessories awaited discovery. The fun was opening it and being surprised at which one you got.

We waited to give it to you until Pearl had been checked in and opened it for you, allowing you to sprinkle the pieces of a house painter into your hands. A head, a hat, a paint splattered torso and legs and a paint roller in two parts. The Decorator!

As you assembled it, something clicked. Pun very much intended. That single figure kept you entertained for hours.

Meanwhile Pearl, you were starting what would be a four-day stay at the hospital to fight the sudden infection. I doubt you'll ever forget the experience as you experienced trauma and pain there. But there were moments of care and joy.

Mom slept in the room with you every night and barely spent a minute away from you. You weren't contagious so lots of our friends and their kids came to visit. A musician came one day and played songs on the guitar for you. A nurse spent an entire hour and a half next to the bed with you watching a movie, so we could take a break and get some lunch. Later she explained she had chosen her job because one of her own kids had spent so much time in hospitals and she knew the difference she could make for patients during a long stay.

And one afternoon a cart was wheeled into your room brimming with toys. You were instructed to take one and your eyes went right for the big pink plastic box full of Lego, dumping them out onto your hospital bed and putting them together in all sorts of shapes and combinations. You were hooked too.

You guys both skipped right over the Duplo phase and started on the real stuff from day one.

Lego rose to the top of every Christmas and birthday wish list. The basement playroom and your bedrooms were filled with tiny colored bricks and little people in varying states of completion.

We quickly discovered Oregon was home to one, and eventually several, Bricks and Minifigs stores that sold both new and used sets. Lego catalogs started arriving in the mail and could occupy hours of time. Shelves began to fill with completed and Frankensteined sets.

A few years later we planned a trip to Los Angeles to see friends and family, and decided to end the trip with a visit to Legoland.

Inspired by a friend of Susan's, we decided not to tell you guys about the plan. Instead, pretending it was time to go to the airport, we used an iPhone to take a video of your reaction when you realized we were actually turning into the Legoland theme park.

Honesty, we were expecting and even hoping for whoops and hollers. Instead you both just stared out the windows, mouths agape. As you later explained, Pearl, you were both so surprised you were literally speechless. You couldn't believe we were there. The whoops and hollers came over the next two days as we explored and enjoyed every inch of the park.

For years, Pearl, you really led the Lego play. You loved building scenes and creating worlds.

When you were seven, you decided that Lego should come out with a Scooby-Doo series of sets, Scooby-Doo being one of your own, Everett and Mom's all-time and enduring favorite shows.

You were so invested in the idea you decided to write a letter to the Lego Corporation. Your first, and for many years, only letter you ever wrote. You made a compelling argument and you even addressed it and added the return address and stamp yourself.

And lo and beyond a few months later, five Scooby Doo sets were released.

Naturally those sets had been in development before the letter, but we weren't going to let on, and that Christmas the sets were under the tree.

Eventually you moved onto other passions, Pearl. But Lego has remained an interest. You loved the Lego Masters TV show, even into your teen years. And you've always been up for a visit to the Lego store, campaigning for as big a budget as you could get from us, only to give all of it to Everett to spend once we got there.

Everett, you got into Lego and just went deeper and deeper and deeper. I imagine you have no less than a hundred different sets.

And you have gone through many, many different phases.

You had a city phase when you were most interested in fire trucks, police cars and bank robbers. You've had super hero phases, knight and castle phases, several Minecraft phases and many more Star Wars phases.

I can remember when you went from slowly talking about your sets and turning them into something else entirely into keeping them intact, ready for future play.

And when visits to the Lego store evolved from big budget affairs where you spent birthday money on entire sets to more recently going with a small budget and spending two hours picking out the perfect set of specialized bricks and tiny accessories.

But the constant has been your fascination with mini-figures.

The Lego Movie hinged on the idea that there are two types of Lego builders. Those who follow the instructions and keep sets true to their original designs and those who use Lego to create their own inventions.

I would argue there are also those that build structures and vehicles and spaceships out of bricks, and others who tell stories using those things and their mini-figs.

Everett, you are decidedly the latter.

I can't fully know what's going through your head when you play with Lego. But I have seen you watch a TV show and then immediately spend the next hour creating your own narratives with Lego.

I have seen play acting with your Lego, creating dialogue and elaborate situations, and I suspect it's been how you process events and social situations from your own life. Or maybe you're writing entirely new stories, entire novels, in your head.

For me the added bonus beyond seeing you guys on the ground happily playing without a screen in sight, is that it's given me a reason to join in and play with toys again alongside you.

Sometimes, Everett, you've asked me to build a new set while you put the mini-figures together. Or build you a castle, which was my favorite thing to build as a kid.

For a while we'd have drafts and each assemble an entire armada of boats and warriors and then have a battle on your blue rug that you'd always inevitably win.

Lego has also been a way to connect with friends and family.

One of your all-time favorite gifts, Everett, was when your cousin Julian sent you his old Lego for Christmas. The prize was a mostly complete Indiana Jones set that provided months of enjoyment before it morphed and evolved piece by piece into something else entirely.

And Lego has been the surest way for you to bond with your younger cousin James, who has a particular fondness for cars and trucks. When we visit DC to see him, Alex, Caitlyn and now Ellis (who is one and a half as of this writing), you three will disappear downstairs and set up ramps and jumps for his Lego vehicles to navigate and collide into each other.

And even during the pandemic, when Lego became more essential than ever, I got a text one morning from my cousin Alexis. It was a picture of a spaceship her son Hugo had built and wanted you to see, Everett. Because even years after meeting you, he remembered how much you loved Lego.

For months you two would send pictures of strange and cool things you made back and forth.

It's hard for me to imagine your life with Lego, but I suspect some lean years will come. As you get older they will become less something you play with, more something you look at. And when you head off to college or out into the "real world" as we used to say, they might end up in boxes down in the basement or up in our eaves.

I promise you this.

Your mom and I won't ever sell or give them away. We'll also find somewhere to store them.

Because I'm confident one day when you're older, maybe with your own kids or just feeling like you want to be a kid again yourself, you'll come back home and ask for your Lego.

GAME SHOWS

My dad could have won big money if he had paid more attention to kitchens.

He went on a game show called *The Match Game* and was in the lead by show's end and set to win the prize money if got the answer to the last question right.

They had polled the audience beforehand and asked him to try and guess their answer to the question, "What color would most Americans paint their kitchen?"

I'll give you a moment to think what you would have answered. And if it helps this was the early 1960s.

Okay, you got your answer?

Well, if you guessed white you were wrong. That's what your grandfather guessed. The correct answer was yellow. So he didn't win the money, but he won a few hundred bucks. And I think a luggage set.

When I was a kid game shows were on all day long and I loved them, especially the daytime ones because that usually meant I was home sick from school. Watching *The Price is Right* with a low-grade fever was the guilty pleasure of my childhood.

As far as the evening shows *Jeopardy* is arguable the most famous, but it was too hard for me. *Wheel of Fortune* was more my style.

I especially loved watching it with my Grammy Hartman. We'd watch it together on a little black and white TV in her kitchen while she made dinner.

She could almost always solve the puzzle before the contestants. And we loved pretending to shop when the winner of each round chose their prizes.

These days the winner just gets money. Back when I was a kid the show featured a huge rotating carousel divided into three partitions. Each area had a gauntlet of prizes along a theme. So there might be an entire kitchen, with state-of-the-art appliances, fancy cookware and a brand new dinette set. Or it might be vacation themed, with bicycles, camping gear and a Winnebago to shop for. But the winner had to choose super quickly, with the hosts and audience yelling for them to hurry up. So the fun was imagining what we would pick if we were in their shoes but without the pressure.

By the time I was old enough to go on a game show, reality TV had become much more popular than traditional game shows.

MTV was the first network to really embrace the concept, moving from airing music videos to shows like *The Real World* and *Road Rules* by the time I was in college.

Survivor was the first really big reality competition show. It was a primetime event, which is to say it came on at 8pm up against the big network dramas. And strangely your mom and Uncle Alex both had good friends in the first season. Alex's high school friend Colleen was on until halfway through the show, but Susan's friend Kelly made it to the very end and has since reappeared on reunion editions of the show.

I didn't want to go on a reality TV show, but I was fascinated by people who did. Especially a few years into their existence when we really understood what was at stake. Who would want to go on national TV and risk failure, humiliation, or through the power of editing only have their worst self shown? A whole lot of people.

And getting on a show took work. You had to make a video, and then fill out a questionnaire that was dozens of pages long even before auditioning. A couple years after college I found an application for a show online and realized it was a psychological test to figure out how you worked with other people and reacted to stress.

Only the producers of reality TV shows weren't screening out people who were likely to fall apart under the pressure, or blame other people for their own mistakes. They were casting those people because they created the conflict and drama that made people want to tune in and keep watching.

I was making my own films at the time (remember, from the end of the *Baseball Cards* chapter), and had begun creating characters for my friend and myself to play. So I decided to invent a character who would be irresistible catnip for reality TV producers.

I hit the tanning salon, got a flat top, frosted my tips, bought a black jean jacket and a button up shirt with a dragon printed across the chest and rented a massive SUV. I became Hunter Dawson, a brash Southern Californian "bro" out of step with laid-back, quietly-judging, hipper-than-thou Portland.

My friend and regular collaborator Steve MacDougall followed me around town with a camera, filming and directing the action as I rolled into restaurants and bars unannounced and interacted with people in character as Hunter. To ensure the film had a story arc we cast a few plants for some key scenes, including your mom, who played a bar patron thoroughly uninterested in talking to me. Then we edited together what would become Hunter's "blanket application video."

In the finished film Hunter came out of the gate strong, acting like he owned Portland. But pretty soon his social isolation became apparent and by video's end he was confessing how lonely he was and how badly he needed to be on a reality TV show to escape his life.

When the film was done I submitted it to a bunch of film festivals and it screened at a bunch of "underground" film festivals who understood it was satire. But I also sent VHS tapes along with a personal note with my phone number on garish full-color Hunter Dawson stationary to reality TV shows. And a few took the bait.

The producers of *Fear Factor* were particularly interested in casting Hunter, calling me several times. The show format consisted of people competing in challenges like eating live insects, and crawling from the roof of a car into the driver's seat in order to start the engine, only suspended on a crane two hundred feet in the air.

I was excited they kept calling, doing my best to switch from my regular phone voice to Hunter's when they did, but I had no interest in going on the show. I'm not big into eating live insects and I was worried I might break character halfway into being hoisted hundreds of feet in the air and start screaming for help.

It was enough for me to fool them into thinking Hunter was real. Or maybe they saw right through me and didn't care. I read an article in the *Village Voice* around that time by a reporter who lied about who he was to appear as a guest on a daytime talk show for his piece. He assumed everyone else was "real." Then he saw one of the guests from his show playing a completely different person on another talk show and found out she and most of the other guests were actors looking to keep their craft sharp.

I also didn't want to be in front of a national audience with someone else in control of how I was portrayed, even if I would be in character. Which makes me a bit of an anomaly.

People used to value privacy. Who you voted for was often a secret. These days try and find someone who won't tell every friend of their friend's friend who they are voting for and why you should too.

I think reality TV played a pivotal role in that shift. For the first time anyone could become famous. You didn't have to be rich or talented. You just had to be you. And then Facebook came along and gave everyone with a smartphone a platform to keep their friends "followers" informed of their every meal and move.

I have tried to help you two understand there is such a thing as too much information, especially when it comes to what you share with the world.

And I'm already seeing encouraging signs.

Pearl, I appreciate your deep mistrust and suspicion of social media, especially as you've seen how it's consumed and affected friends and classmates who got a head start. And Everett, I can't imagine you'll keep your complete disinterest in social media bordering on obliviousness forever. But I hope we can keep it that way for a little while longer.

Just try and promise me you won't go on reality TV. No good can come of it. What they don't tell you is how many of the people who went on Survivor came home with parasites or the ways contestants are manipulated into doing things they don't want to do.

But I'm okay with you going on a game show. There's usually just a question or two you answer at the start of the show about yourself and then it's off to answering trivia questions, or guessing what other people paint their kitchens or whatever the premise is. And you might even win some money. Or some luggage.

CLUBS

Growing up my brother and I had the immense fortune of spending the summer in a sprawling summer house called the BeeHive in Weld, Maine.

It belonged to my mom's childhood neighbors, the Wests. They stayed there every August, but rented it to our family for the five or six weeks before. We went every year, year after year, and it was awesome.

The house wasn't winterized so when we showed up we were the first people to step foot in it since the previous summer. We'd walk around the house first and then cautiously open the front door. There was no telling what damage the long Maine winter had done, or if a family of small mammals had moved in. But once cleaned and swept of creatures, it was on.

The BeeHive was aptly named. My parents had an open house policy and invited friends and family to come stay. There were days when a minivan would pull away and a new one would pull in an hour later and cooped-up kids and vacation-hungry parents would spill out, ready for fun. And if guests overlapped, that was fine. The second floor was a labyrinth of bedrooms and bunk beds.

After folks came and stayed with us, they'd often rent their own place nearby the next summer, which only made the cocktail hours and lobster dinners bigger and better over time. We almost always hosted, as the BeeHive had a long dining room table that could seat over a dozen adults, and a screened in porch with two tables that could accommodate as many kids.

I loved having all those guests coming and going, especially my cousins, Chris, Amanda, and Peter, who were around the same age as my brother and me. They would stay with us along with their parents, while my Grammy Dickson would rent her own place just down the road.

The BeeHive sat on a small hill across a gravel road from a field that had a pathway going down to the sandy beach and clear blue water of Lake Webb. It's one of those picture-book lakes with blue mountains behind it that makes the water look emerald green by comparison. Idyllic doesn't even do it justice.

For a month, that was our world. There was no school or soccer practices. This was of course before the internet and we couldn't get any channels on the black and white TV so we'd store it in the closet. In town there were some tennis courts, a general store and the aptly and amazingly named "The Other Store." A real grocery store or movie theater was half an hour away. You had to make your own fun.*

My cousins and your uncle Alex and I would spend all day in pack formation, running down to the lake to play Marco Polo or swim out to "the big rock" whose surface was just a few feet underwater, so you could stand on it and wave back to shore. There was a forest of giant ferns off to the side of the beach path that was perfect for real-life Dungeons & Dragons, which we would play with paper and books on the porch whenever it rained. In the evening we'd lie in the yard on our backs and shoot pieces of bread into the sky with slingshots for the bats to swoop down and eat.

There was also a tiny little cabin on the property called the Matchbox, which had its own driveway parallel to the wide area where minivans came and went to access the BeeHive. To create the illusion of privacy there was a thin corridor of trees and bushes separating the two. It was just wide enough to create a club house.

We called it the Hot Bee Club. Maybe because someone got stung by a bee? On a hot day?

The most important order of our club business was making fun of each other. Chris was a master at this. He had one song he sang about me being a string bean because I was skinny. He gave my brother Alex a sing-song nickname that would set him off every time he heard it. And being the oldest, he knew exactly how to get under the skin of his siblings Amanda and Peter.

Alex made an especially easy target because once he got really laughing he physically could not stop. Since the club was about making jokes, that spelled doom for

Alex. It would get to the point where you could just say his name and it would send him further into hysterics.

But I think your Uncle Alex was just vocalizing how we all felt. Free and like having fun was our full-time job. A picture from the time shows the five of us, crowded onto a small dock on Lake Webb, the full membership of the Hot Bee Club. We're all making faces, laughing our heads off.

Meanwhile, the adults were conducting meetings of their own club inside.

My parents and their friends Bob and Monica Skole got this idea for creating an organization called C-Note. I don't think they had any official business other than conducting official business. So there were by-laws, and documents of creation, but I think the whole thing was kind of a send-up of bureaucracy and an excuse to have boozy meetings and get some swag made.

They ordered C-Note mugs, bought cheap trucker hats and embroidered them with a C-Note patch, and even had branded foam drink koozies made.

Much to our chagrin they ordered Hot Bee Club swag too! Probably because they thought the name was so funny.

We were horrified when we were each presented with our individualized Hot Bee Club t-shirt, complete with each of our names on the back. We thought we were being secretive and couldn't believe they all knew about it. But the Hot Bee Club survived this indignity and lasted a few more summers.

When I look back on my childhood I have about as many memories from the month we spent in Maine every summer as the other eleven months combined.

Vacation can expose you to different cultures and ideas and people. But going somewhere different can also just take you out of your day to day life and transport you somewhere new. And they are a great way to pinpoint moments in your life.

Even now when I try to think back on a previous year, it's the vacations we took as a family or trips I went on that help me remember what we do, what happened and where my strongest memories come from.

A big part of why I moved to Oregon is because it feels a lot like Maine. I'm a city person, as if your mom, so we each chose Portland on our own before meeting here. But I think we were both drawn to the Pacific Northwest because there is a lifetime of adventures and vacations just a short drive away.

Your mom and I have tried to give you the kind of experiences where you can escape regular life for a while. Every time we book a cabin up near Mt. Hood, rent a beach house out on the Coast, or stay on Wallowa Lake out in Eastern Oregon, we're trying to offer you two your chance to run in your own pack formation, find other kids to hang out with, invent new games and revisit old ones.

If you have a family of your own someday, or even if you don't, do your best to switch things up and travel as much as you can. You don't have to go on a big International trip, although those are nice. Even an overnight adventure or a long day trip can break up life as usual, give you new things to see and experience, and create a milemarker that you'll long remember and look back on fondly.

*As I mentioned, there wasn't much in the way of a community gathering place in Weld. No big public park or popular beach. But there was one place where you could run into most of the town on a Friday night. The dump.

By day, folks drove their trash to the dump and threw it off a steep cliff to join the rest of the trash. But on cool summer nights folks brought coolers of drinks and set up lawn chairs. Dozens of people would be there, sitting and catching up on the latest gossip right above the valley of garbage, never mind the powerful aroma. Then a hush would fall over the crowd as the local family of bears came out to scavenge for food down below.

BOOKS

There is such a thing as too much of anything. Except books.

When I was a kid we'd go visit our friends the O'Briens. Their kids John and Beth were the same age as Alex and I, with very similar interests, and our parents got along really well, so it always felt like a party, even if it was just the eight of us.

They lived in a rowhouse in Washington, DC near the Capitol where we'd go every few months for dinner. The house was narrow but deep, and rose four stories off the ground. They had a spiral staircase towards the back of the house, and a staircase near the front rising steeply from the street level all the way up to the attic. So it was the perfect house for hide and seek, tag, and other imagination games.

My favorite part of their house was a series of bookshelves at the top of the first landing covered floor to ceiling with art books. Tall, thick coffee table books about sculpture and painting and theater. I tried to comprehend the time and money it would take to collect all those books. It seemed impossible. But I wanted them.

We had a lot of books around our house too, here, there almost everywhere you looked. After all, my Dad, your grandfather, is a writer and a collector.

He got his start writing after the Navy writing magazine articles, and then took a series of jobs at trade magazines. He loved being assigned an article about something he knew nothing about, because the research was as much fun for him as the writing.

I believe the first book he wrote was a mystery for kids but he couldn't find a publisher. So he wrote a book called *Think Tanks*, I presume about Think Tanks. (Sorry Dad, I never read that one.) Quickly followed by *the Great American Ice Cream Book*, which I did read. And he just kept going, writing about a book a year until well after I was grown up and you guys were born.

He wrote joke books, word books, baseball books and even one about libraries. He was also especially interested in language and started compiling a list of synonyms for the word drunk, thinking that thanks to authors like Shakespeare, it would have more than any other word.

Eventually he submitted the list to *the Guinness Book of World Records* and they created a new category, "most synonyms for a word" and included it in their book. A year later someone else beat it by adding two more words to his list, so he found two dozen more and took the record back. He was quite proud of that.

One of his most successful books was *The Official Rules*, a collection of Murphy's Laws. Like "the other line always moves faster." He put our address in the back and encouraged people to send them their Murphy's Law.

And sure enough, we'd go to the post office and get letters from people all over the country sharing their own rules. He published two more books filled up with crowd-sourced submissions. Before the Internet!

As he got older he kept going, writing longer books that took a few years each to research and write. He wrote about Sputnik, and another called *The Bonus Army* and he returned to baseball, writing two biographies. And even published a book about the secret beginning of World War II called *The Rise of the G.I. Army* when he was 80.

I say my Dad wrote these books and his name is on the jacket. But your grandmother was there with him every step of the way. She was his collaborator on ideas, his in-house editor and proofreader, and was often the business manager as well. She actually left a full-time job to take over the family finances and immediately discovered a publisher was holding out on thousands of dollars. I can close my eyes and hear her talking on the phone patiently but firmly explaining to the finance department of a magazine that the check for an article is long overdue, and asking when exactly it will be mailed.

Your mom is also a writer. I'd like to say it's partly what made me fall in love with her but she wasn't doing a lot of writing when we met. She was making jewelry. Initially metal-smithing and then beading. Then she taught herself to sew and started making handbags and skirts.

Pretty soon she was selling her line Susan Stars in stores across the country and even founded a craft collective with a few other women. They made a website where Susan started writing articles and craft tutorials and a publisher reached out. Would they like to write a book? Yes they would.

Each member of the collective contributed lots of projects to make, but being a great writer and communicator Susan did a lot of the work to connect them all together.

One fun side note is that when they needed an illustrator, they put up an ad on Craigslist and got lots of submissions. They picked a guy named Ryan Berkley who drew them as superheroes for the cover, along with lots of instructional illustrations for inside the book. Flash forward a few years and he quit his job to work on his art full time. His Berkley Illustration animal portraits are so popular that when Etsy went public, they flew him out to the New York Stock Exchange to ring the opening bell.

Susan loved co-writing the book so much that she found an agent and wrote another book called *Bead Simple*. And then another called *Button it Up* and then another, and another, and another. She's up to 9 now and has a new proposal she's very excited about.

What amazes me about your mom is her ability to get interested in something and go from novice to master in a matter of months if not weeks.

She went from sewing her first-ever quilt to publishing a book called *Modern Log Cabin Quilting* just a few years later, with her stunning Modern Crosses quilt on the cover which people all over the world have made for themselves.

Your childhood was filled with days when she woke up with an idea, and went down to her sewing room only to come up hours later with an entirely brand new beautiful creation. The floorboards of our house are sturdy, but sound carries through them, so I'm sure you can close your eyes and hear her humming along with her sewing machine purring.

As for me, I never wanted to be a writer because that's what my Dad did. I liked the idea of doing something different. So I made films for a while and then became a performer. But I couldn't resist the urge to write.

First it was screenplays, and then the scripts for my own performances. Which eventually led to my job as a copywriter writing taglines, manifestos and TV commercials for companies like Apple and Adidas.

And I too have published a few books of my own. I wrote a couple different zines back in the day. I co-wrote the second edition of Alexander Barrett's book *This is Portland*, adding several new essays to expand the book and earn a co-credit. And I got to write a book for Wieden+Kennedy, which first required me to travel around the world with a designer I was partnered with to visit and learn about each office. We went from Portland to New York to London to Amsterdam to Delhi to Shanghai to Tokyo and then home.

The best way to become a better writer is to read a lot. And we've done our best to keep books all around you. I think it's safe to say we've succeeded.

Your mom and I met here in Portland, then moved down to Los Angeles a few years later. We moved back intending to start a family and were lucky enough to be able to buy a house. The one we bought is the house you know.

It kind of looks like a house a kindergartener would draw on the outside, but has some fun and beautiful mid-century touches on the inside. We fell in love with all the details. The cup and toothbrush holder in our pink princess bathroom below the mirror that swings around to a shiny mirror back. And the cozy wood-paneled rooms with sloped eaves on the second floor which are your bedrooms.

But the moment I knew we'd be moving in is when we walked through the kitchen and went down the stairs into the basement. I could stand up straight! A rarity given my height and the low ceilings and tight feel of most Portland basements. And then, across a wide open area, was a door leading to what's now our vast finished rec room. With a fireplace, a handmade bar, checkerboard tile floor and empty walls waiting for bookshelves.

We bought and built bookshelves, got all our books out of storage, and before you knew it we had our own floor-to-ceiling walls of books. Art books, craft books, cook books, so many novels and of course the books your grandfather and mom have written.

Sometimes I go downstairs to the rec room and sit on the couch and just look up at all our books. There aren't a lot of things I've always wanted but walls of books are one of them, and I feel so fortunate that we have them.

And I know you both appreciate having books everywhere you turn.

Everett, anytime you've expressed an interest in a book or series we go all in. I believe you've read every Calvin and Hobbes, every Big Nate, and while it's impossible to read every Archie and Betty and Veronica double digest comic ever written, we track them down in lots on eBay so you can give it your best try.

Pearl you've gone from reading kids books to young adult to teen and now are more likely to read an adult book then any else. And you delight in reading kids the books we used to read you to your cousins and when you babysit.

And from a very young age, you've written your own books. Sometimes you write alone, but you've just as happy to write with friends. At the time of this writing you've got a book in progress, which you're reimagining despite already being five thousand words in, and are working on your first screenplay.

You both have such great imaginations, such strong opinions, and such a vast and wide vocabulary. Everett, thanks to your love of old Mad magazines and Bloom County, I think you know more about 1980s politics and pop culture than most of us who actually lived through it.

That's all to say I know you two will have your own stories to tell. Maybe they'll take book form. I not so secretly hope they do. But whatever form they take, I can't wait to hear them.

ICE CREAM

The first time my mom met her future in-laws they took her to dinner at their country club. She ordered an ice cream sundae for dessert, took a big bite and felt something crunch in her mouth. Turns out it was glass. She didn't say anything at first, but when her mouth started to bleed she came clean.

Even still, it didn't diminish her lifelong love of ice cream.

Growing up we had dessert immediately after dinner seven days a week. Sometimes dessert was cantaloupe, but more often it was ice cream. We usually had a few flavors to choose from and there was often homemade pound cake or strawberries to go with it. Both if we were lucky.

As you two well know and love, even now when we all visit my parents there are four or five cartons of ice cream in the freezer.

Your grandpa is also a big ice cream fan, so much so he wrote a book about it. It's a mix of his own ice cream odyssey and an ice-cream centric take on world history. He posits that Christopher Columbus set off to find the new world to bring ice back to Spain to allow the royal court to enjoy ice cream.

Peach was my Dad's favorite flavor, I think mostly because it gave him a chance to remind us it is the hardest flavor to make. Apparently freezing peaches without them turning rock hard is a tricky business. My mom was more of a chocolate fan. Alex was all about mint chocolate chip. And my favorite was the German chocolate cake you could only get at Baskin Robbins.

Most of the year we ate our ice cream from the carton, but every summer when we'd travel up to Maine and eat our ice cream out of a cone courtesy of the Weld Inn.

The Inn was just up the hill and across the main road from the BeeHive, the sprawling summer house we rented every July. And we made that walk frequently after dinner.

The Inn was seldom in good enough shape for overnight guests. But every summer at the end of the long white front porch, illuminated by a lively fluorescent bug zapper that kept the mosquitoes at bay, the ice cream window was open for business,

There were usually two or three people working, but we'd all try and angle our place in line so that Larry would take our order and scoop our cone. He was a teenager with huge forearms so when he scooped a single it was as big as a Baskin Robbins triple.

The walk to and from the Inn was short but often eventful. There was the time my Dad had one of us up on his shoulders, lost his footing and sacrificed his knee in order to prevent an injury to his child or his own cone.

Another time we were walking back home with some friends staying with us and we were attacked by a colony of bees. Adults were swatting bees off of screaming kids as they were getting stung themselves. One even went right up my Dad's nose and stung him there.

All of a sudden a woman came out of nowhere with some homemade compound she had created and gave us each some to make the swelling go down and the stings feel better. I have no idea what was in there, but it worked. We had never seen her and never saw her again.

Still we kept going up the hill for ice cream, night after night, summer after summer.

So I'd have to say ice cream was our biggest food tradition as a family. I remember enjoying it with my grandparents, aunts, uncles and cousins. Even Grandma Jeanie, who is now lactose intolerant, always has a few pints of sorbet on hand. Which I'd argue is in the ice cream extended family.

And I'm happy that the two of you are doing your part and then some to carry on our ice cream-loving tradition. While you're arguably not living through the best of the times, you are living in the golden age of ice cream. *The New York Times* recently ran a story saying so.

You are especially lucky ice cream wise as Oregon is home to local brands like Umpqua and Tillamook, and Portland is full of several scoop shops that make their own, the most famous being Salt & Straw. They started as a single shop and on the strength of contemporary flavors like Salted Caramel and Honey Lavender (your favorite, Everett) quickly expanded across the city and up and down the West Coast. You can even find Salt & Straw at Disneyland.

People love it because they make so many different, unexpected, and unusual flavors. As you know I did some work for them off and on for a while and part of my job was writing the flavor descriptions for their menu. I'd get on the phone with the ice cream maker in chief and I'd ask him three questions about each new flavor. Where did the idea come from? How do you make it? And what does it taste like? The last one being quite important as they often didn't have it ready for me to try yet.

It would take him ten full minutes to answer those three questions for a single new flavor. Once we had 25 new flavors to go over so I spent the entire day listening, scribbling down notes.

They are also a good company, giving money where money should go and they have a cool program where they visit the public elementary school closest to each of their Portland shops and do a little show and tell, complete with ice cream tasting. Then they announce a contest where kids can invent their own flavor of ice cream.

Pearl, you were lucky enough to be part of that experience and dutifully submitted an idea every year.

When you were in 3rd grade, you submitted a flavor called "It's Raining Kit-Kat's and Chocolate Scotties." Very clever, but I suspect the raining cats and dogs reference wasn't a quick-enough get. So that year, other kids' flavors were declared the winners.

Undeterred, you came back in 4th grade and focusing on flavor and ingredients you submitted a flavor called Tacocat. The rules required you to submit a description and yours read "a delicious Mexican vanilla ice cream, with stirred in crumbled Mexican chocolate, tortilla chips, queso fresco, and a sprinkle of mild chili powder plus a pinch of cinnamon."

That's some pretty sophisticated flavor profiling for a nine-year old. Neither Mom or I were quite sure where you came up with it. But we were proud.

Lo and behold, it was one of the three winning submissions from your school. Not only did that bring prestige, they actually made Tacocat into a real ice cream and served it at our neighborhood shop all month long!

Oh, the fanfare. You got to visit their ice cream factory and see them make a batch of your flavor. You and the other winners from around the city were invited onto a morning TV talk show. Best of all was seeing your pride at walking into the store, and explaining to the folks working the counter you were the Pearl who invented Tacocat as you ordered your own scoop.

And here's the thing. It was good!

It tasted really, really good. We still have a few freezer-burnt pints of it at the very back of our freezer. They are inedible at this point, but I'm not sure if we can ever bear to throw them out.

CALIFORNIA

The two biggest constellations in the solar system of my family were New York and California. Growing up we saw New York up close regularly, where most of my Dad's side of the family lived. But California, where most of my mom's family lived, I could only imagine as if through a telescope. Or more accurately the telephone.

My mom, your Grammy Dickson, grew up on Long Island, New York in a town called Sea Cliff. When she and her older brother Charlie were both in college, her parents moved to Southern California with her younger brother Dick.

Her parents moved back a few years later, but Dick never left. He's lived in the Silver Lake neighborhood of Los Angeles for the last fifty years and counting. It's where he met his wife Leslie, and raised their three kids, my cousins Erica, Ian, and Stephen.

Dick loved to talk on the telephone. He called us at least once a week and insisted on talking to every one of us, Which was good for Alex and I. It made us less shy and more used to speaking to the many adults who were always calling our house. My oldest cousin Erica caught the phone bug too, and would call us all by herself when she was a little kid without her parents knowing. After a while my mom would have to politely say goodbye, as these were back in the days when long distance calls were charged by the minute.

My mom's older brother Uncle Charlie has lived all over. New York, Spain, Florida, and Paris just to name a few. He's lived in California several times and started both his families there.

His first wife Lela spent most of her life in Carmel, as did their son, my oldest cousin Michael. Charlie's second wife Joan spent most of her life in Silver Lake too, as did their daughter, my younger cousin Alexis.

I didn't get to see much of Dick and Leslie or any of the cousins on my mom's side growing up. We never made it out to California, and they only came East one or twice. But I saw a lot of Uncle Charlie.

He would come to visit us once a year or so. Usually for a long stretch. Whenever I asked my parents how long he was staying, they would say they didn't know. Even as a kid I could tell he didn't really have anywhere to go and was figuring out his next move.

It could put a strain on my parents, but I enjoyed it when he came to stay. He treated Alex and I more like younger brothers than nephews. Less a third parent, more "hey, what's that on your shirt? Made you look."

Charlie was an idea guy, and always had a big film or publishing project he was working on. And he was a great "opener," so he could talk his way into almost any room and could sell almost anyone on his ideas.

One time he moved to Spain to try and make a film commemorating the 500th anniversary of Columbus "discovering" America. Quotes because you both know America didn't need discovering; people were already living here.

My parents were dubious. It's not like he had a major studio or even a minor one backing him. But one day we got a letter from him telling us the Spanish government loved the idea and was in for half a million dollars. He even included a picture of him shaking hands with the King of Spain to prove it. They were both grinning towards the camera.

The problem was Charlie wasn't as strong of a closer. So a lot of his wonderful ideas, like the Columbus film, never came to fruition. But it never stopped him from trying again and again. He always had another big idea at the ready. And his passion absolutely inspired me.

I moved to Portland after college to make my own movies. I had always been excited by the idea of movie-making, and had majored in film in college.

Moving West meant the orbit of the family I saw shifted. My Dad's side of the family was now all the way across the country, but Mom's side was close.

My cousin Erica came up to visit Portland on a road trip with a friend soon after I moved here. Around that same time, Alex came out to visit and we took the train down to Oakland and met our cousin Michael for an A's baseball game. Then we spent the night at a vineyard owned by a friend of his in California wine country.

Just before you two came along, your mom and I moved down to Los Angeles for a few years. We moved there mostly for my career ambitions. Your mom was up for the adventure and already had lots of friends down that way from the craft community.

I was trying to sell screenplays to Hollywood with my friend Bill Bailey, and maybe pick up a little acting work as well. As if it were laying around for anyone to pick and take.

We got as far as landing a manager and an entertainment lawyer. But not as far as selling a script for them to manage or negotiate. But we did get to spend time with my family.

We caught up with my cousin Alexis and her partner Andrew a lot as they lived close by. Alexis is a wonderful illustrator and she ended up collaborating with your Mom for years, illustrating a good handful of her craft books.

My Uncle Dick and Aunt Leslie especially loved having us near. Family is the most important thing in the world to them, and their kids have almost always lived close by. They picked your mom and I up a few times and drove us all over the greater Los Angeles area, showing us little towns and hidden canyons. The Southern California you never see on TV or hear about.

That was what struck me most about living in Los Angeles. It might make you think of luxury and fame. But even Hollywood is a place full of all kinds of different people mostly doing regular kinds of things.

Naturally we did have a few "Hollywood" moments.

My screenwriting partner Bill Bailey and I spent a few months writing a screenplay for a production company on the Sony lot. And the thrill of driving up to the gates of a major studio, giving your names and seeing the gate rise and the guard waving you through never gets old.

Your mom and I were cast in a music video for the band Bright Eyes that was set on an airplane. The director was an old friend, so she put us in the seats just in front of the video's two stars, Terance Stamp and Evan Rachel Wood. So we're on camera for a surprising amount of the video. Yes, you can YouTube it.

And we ran into our fair share of celebrities at movie theaters, farmer's markets and the Hollywood flea markets. Yet it was the everyday stuff that was the most fun of all.

I think that's why your mom had a better time than I did. She made new friends and took the subway to the fabric and jewelry supply districts in downtown LA, where she found all kinds of treasures to incorporate into projects for her books. She wasn't trying to "make it" in Los Angeles. She approached it as a place to live, and it is those experiences that stand out most.

A few evenings every week we'd leave our tiny Los Feliz apartment, cross Franklin, and wind our way through the Hollywood Hills to hike up the trails to Griffith Observatory. If the sky was clear we could see all the way to the Pacific Ocean.

We also really started to explore food together. We lived a short walk from dozens of Thai restaurants, and tried them all before settling on a favorite.

We went out for dim sum regularly in Chinatown, got amazing taqueria tacos at the car wash, and fell in love with an ahi tuna-sesame seed dish at our favorite restaurant The Kitchen that was so good, we each ordered a full entree every time we went.

But the best meals were the ones we had with my mom's whole side of the family when my parents came to visit. It was great to finally see my mom and her brothers, with her nieces and nephews, all sharing the same table. It was never anywhere fancy. Just breakfast at a place with massive omelets and complimentary muffins. Or an Italian restaurant that could have been anywhere but Italy.

Regular places.

Everett, I can't imagine you'll ever live in Los Angeles, although I could be wrong. Your friend Jag lives down there, and a friend is often reason enough to move somewhere.

Pearl, I can't imagine you won't live in either Los Angeles, New York City or both at some point in your life. I know you have big dreams. And I think you'll achieve them. Just remember to enjoy the everyday stuff, like the dim sum, or in your case the sushi, along the way.

EBAY

The two of you come from a long line of collectors and garage sale enthusiasts.

Your great-grandmother on my Dad's side was an art and antique collector. Your Great-Uncle Dick was a record dealer and spent years with his wife Leslie selling their wares at the Orange Country Flea Market. And your mom is of course a collector of vintage buttons, fabric, quilts, handbags, and more.

Growing up, we could not pass by a garage sale without stopping. My Dad was a big collector and a self-described wheeler and dealer. He loved junk shops and antique stores but flea markets were his favorite.

When we visited my mom's parents in Florida every spring, we would make a pilgrimage to a flea market the size of a small town. There were rows and rows of booths to explore, each with two dozen vendors on either side.

It was so vast that when my brother and I set out to look for baseball cards and comic books, we needed to set a meeting time and place so we could find our parents again.

My dad had a few things he was always on the prowl for. Marbles, stereo views and mechanical pens and pencils were just a few of his areas of interest and expertise.

One time he bought a collection of old pens and pencils from one dealer for fifty dollars, took out the best ones and then sold everything else to another dealer for a hundred bucks. That blew me away. Before that, I took it as fact that dealers always got the best of you.

The baseball card worth twenty dollars in the price guide was only worth six if you were hoping to sell it at the local card shop. Maybe eight if you were willing to take store credit. But my Dad danced with the dealers and won.

I got the collector bug when I was young, amassing a large collection of baseball cards and then comic books. But in high school my collecting turned off like a switch. I got more into listening to music and hanging out with friends.

When I moved to Portland after college I noticed there were estate sales and thrift stores everywhere. Rather than go out and buy new clothes or furniture it just made sense to find old stuff. It was cooler, often better made, and way more affordable. Plus there was the thrill of the hunt.

Your mom loves thrift shopping as well, so when we met we spent a lot of time roaming the aisles of second hand stores. Saturday mornings we'd circle estate sale listings in the paper we planned on visiting that afternoon, or better yet Sunday when everything was half off.

We knew some of what we were finding was valuable, but selling what we found never really occurred or appealed to us.

At the time I was working in the film industry, going on coffee runs as a production assistant, and then later moving furniture and props as a union set dresser. The money was decent, but I was either working fourteen-hour days for weeks on end, or not working at all. It made making plans or showing up to band practice hard. So I was looking for something a little more stable without actually doing any looking.

My parents kept telling me about a new website called eBay.

I resisted the Internet strongly at first. I was dimly aware of email in college, but with so many new people to meet and a phone down at the end of the hall the idea of writing someone on the computer didn't make any sense.

So even in my mid-twenties I still didn't have an internet connection. When Susan and I wanted to go online or check our new email accounts, we went to the library.

But the unpredictable hours of film production continued to take a toll, and my parents kept talking up the online sales they were making from my Dad's antique marbles, pencils and pens.

So one day I bought a modem, plugged my computer up to the phone line at our apartment, and there it was, eBay. An online flea market, with folks from all over the world bidding on everything you could imagine. It was great for dealers, since they could now reach a broader audience, but what made eBay awesome was regular people could buy and sell with each other, and get top dollar on the one hand, and find exactly what they wanted on the other.

So you could actually get twenty dollars for that baseball card a dealer would only give you six bucks for. Or even thirty if two people got in a bidding war. And that rare card, or vintage lunch box or whatever it was you had been searching years for? You didn't even have to leave your living room to find it.

Susan and I started walking those thrift store aisles and estate sale houses looking for stuff to sell.

One of our first big scores was a beautiful vintage western shirt at a rummage sale. The label had a cowgirl sitting on a fence swinging a lasso. The brand was "Nudie." I thought it would make a great gift for my friend Ryan, a songwriter who was singing sad country ballads at the time.

Susan thought it might be worth something. Indeed it was. Nudie made Western wear in the 1960s for cowboys like Roy Rogers, musicians like Elvis and the Beatles and film stars like Ronald Reagan. I put the shirt up on eBay (sorry Ryan) and the Nudie Museum bowed out of the auction at $125. It kept going up. At the last minute there was a bidding war and it sold for $400.

Once my parents saw me making sales, they started sending me some of their overflowing inventory of collectibles.*

My Dad passed along a collection of hundreds of toothpick boxes from the early 1900s. Only they weren't assembled boxes with toothpicks inside.

They were printed proofs, so imagine the box printed on a sheet of cardboard with perforations for edges and folds, but still flat. Yet to be punched out and put together.

My dad had stumbled upon this collection in an antique store in Maine years earlier, and the owner explained that a local printer made most of the toothpick boxes for companies all over the country.

The graphics were incredible, with intricate type and logos depicting baseball players, animals or Santa

Claus. And without fail, a heroic retired dentist-turned-collector would swoop in at the very last minute and win it every single time I put one up for sale. Sometimes one would go for ten bucks, but a Santa Claus-branded box might get bid up to fifty or even a hundred dollars.

After a few months I was making enough money on eBay to quit working in the film business entirely. And around the same time I made the transition in my creative life from being behind the camera to being in front of it.

I had moved to Portland to write and direct my first feature film, hoping it would catapult me to Sundance win and a three-picture deal. I made the film, called *Good Grief*, and it was a fun and rewarding experience. But I realized pretty quickly it was not going to open up a career as a film director. So I took it out on tour for a few months, and then came back and started making little short films with friends.

On a lark I cast myself in the first one, a film about degenerate sports memorabilia dealers, (which you might remember me telling you about earlier in the

Baseball Cards chapter). That experience made me realize how much I liked acting. So I started coming up with film ideas based on different characters I made up.

Pretty soon I realized I didn't have to make a film to play a character. I could just be that character out in the real world or up on stage. It was cheaper, quicker and didn't require an entire crew. And you got to interact with people or the audience, which was half the fun.

Your mom and I were fortunate enough to be asked to be part of the first Time Based Arts (TBA) Festival put on by the Portland Institute for Contemporary Art. The festival was a mix of dance, theater, music and more but the work was always new or rule-breaking or transgressive in some way, with artists and curators coming from all over the world.

We got to do a short piece together where we played dot.com refugee gentrifiers as part of an evening of local performance during the very first festival. Being part of that world left me inspired, mind-blown and wanting to come back and perform at the festival again for the second year with a full-length piece. So I pitched PICA, specifically my friend Erin Boberg, a new show about eBay. And despite my pitch being pretty fuzzy on any details, she said yes!

After spending most of the next year to figure out how to pull it off, your mom and I had a plan.

I would host what felt like a get-rich scheme seminar about the power of eBay, full of fast-talking, cheesy powerpoint slides, audacious boasts and music to work up the crowd. Susan would share the stage bantering back and forth with me, offering up one-liners and working the tech (aka running the PowerPoint presentation) from a podium.

The result was AC Dickson: eBay PowerSeller. The show opened with me running on stage to "Eye of the Tiger," then speaking with a preacher's conviction about the potential of eBay to change lives and even the world.

The show was purportedly about how to sell things on eBay, but we spent the first 45 minutes talking about how revolutionary eBay was. And people really couldn't tell if we were kidding or not.

The finale of the show was watching five real eBay auctions that we had listed a week beforehand close right at the show's finale. And we had the perfect thing to auction off. The toothpick boxes. And I had been saving the best ones for our shows.

So halfway through the show, we'd show the audience that we had some actual eBay items up for bid, ready to end at the close of the show. And the boxes would still be at five or six dollars apiece with half an hour to go.

Then near the end of the show Susan would cue some dance music and pull the auctions back up again, refreshing the browser for their final minute of bidding as I danced the prices up.

Without fail each toothpick box would go from five or six dollars to ten, and then fifty and sometimes even seventy-five or a hundred bucks in a matter of seconds right before their very eyes, thanks to our reliable bidder and collector fending off the competition.

The show really worked. I think because people really weren't sure what we were making up and what was serious. And it didn't really seem like "performance art." Some audience members left thinking this was a big fun joke, while others went home after the show and signed up for eBay accounts.

We had some commercial interest as well. Someone from a company that sold skyscrapers asked if we'd give their sales team a motivation speech. And I got approached by Wieden+Kennedy, the advertising company who coined "Just Do It," about creating a character to pitch to Nike for a series of TV commercials. That would eventually lead to a new career path where I worked for eight years, then an even longer career working as a freelance copywriter.

Best of all, we got to travel with the show.

One of the many benefits of being part of the TBA Festival was that artists and curators came to it from all over the world. And British curators especially loved how American the show felt. We got to tour the show to New York and Victoria, BC, and then to Europe three different times, getting flown there, put up in a hotel, paid a performance fee as well as per diem.

Traveling is great. We have tried to take you two to interesting places and hope your life is full of adventures to new places and different cultures.

But getting paid to travel? And perform? That is the best. I know you hear me, Pearl. You love the stage as much as I do.

The only trouble with traveling with the show was that we were running out of toothpick boxes. If we put anything else up there, even something desirable there was no guarantee it would get bid on at the very last minute, which was part of what made the climax of the show so strong.

What to do?

Well, my parents offered to place a bid on one or two items in the closing minutes. Technically this is an illegal practice called "shill bidding", but we figured a couple extra bucks here or there wouldn't hurt in the name of show business. That said, if you work for eBay... it's been way over seven years! Statute of limitations.

Around this same time, we decided to move to Los Angeles. And once again, collecting and eBay would help.

When I was a kid my parents befriended an elementary school teacher who ran an antique shop during the summer up in Maine to supplement his salary and save up for his kid's college fund. After a string of well-paying articles, my parents had a little money socked away so they asked him if he had something he couldn't sell but might be worth something in the long run.

The teacher slash antique dealer had just the thing. A collection of early American matches and matchboxes from the 1800s. It had come right off the walls of a regional historical society that had closed its doors, so each piece was mounted on heavy cardboard with a thick waxy film encasing it for display. And the entire collective was carefully labeled with dates and descriptions for museum visitors.

Nearly impossible to sell out of a small antique store in the 1980s but perfect for eBay in the 2000s.

When we were getting ready to move, my folks sent us the collection to help. We put it up as individual pieces, about twenty different auctions in total, each for the eBay standard seven-day-long auction.

Within an hour of posting them we had bids totaling about $500. The next day someone emailed offering us $1500 if we took the collection off eBay and sold it directly to them. Sensing we were holding something special we said no.

But the day the auctions were closing I started to question our decision. The collection was still at $500. Then with an hour to go they started to get some more bids. With about 10 minutes to go they were getting even more action, so we called my parents and we all watched the auctions end together, refreshing our browser windows every few seconds to see the new totals. With just a few minutes to go the total was up over two grand.

And then things got really crazy. Every time the page loaded the collection was up hundreds and hundreds of more dollars.

When the dust settled, we hit refresh one last time and saw the collection had sold for eleven thousand dollars.

All but two pieces went to the same high bidder whose personal assistant quickly reached out to handle payment and shipping. We whooped and hollered. It felt like winning the lottery. It was the most money Susan and I had ever had.

But it turns out Los Angeles is expensive and selling screenplays is hard. Pretty soon we had worked through the matchbox money and were living off Susan's book sales and what I was making selling more stuff on eBay.

If you guys are wondering, I still have boxes and boxes of stuff to sell. Vintage bumper stickers, tons of antique postcards, and yes, even a few of those toothpick boxes. So if you guys want to make some money, go for it. I'll even let you use my acdickson account.

* One of my favorite things my parents passed along was a box of antique postcards, most of them from the 1900s, when postcards served the purpose of a more expressive telegram. If you lived in New York City the mail came several times a day. So you could send a postcard asking a friend to dinner in the morning, get a reply mid-day, and send confirmation on where and when to meet late afternoon.

I sold a lot of postcards. Especially when I realized you could often get an entire box of hundreds of rare, antique postcards at an estate sale marked $3 each if you offered $50 cash for the entire lot.

Once I listed a few antique postcards from the Straits Settlements, a territory that included parts of Malaysia and Singapore before their independence from Britain. They went for $700! I couldn't believe it, but the winner explained there were 15 passionate collectors of this era of postcards, mostly living in Japan, Australia, and Malaysia. They all knew each other, and had been excitedly emailing each other about the cards I had listed.

I think that was one of the biggest revelations for me about eBay and the Internet. You can take the most idiosyncratic interest, and there's bound to be a few other people out there as passionate as you. And finally, you could all find each other.

WEDDINGS

The first wedding I saw, I watched from behind the banister of a landing at the top of a flight of stairs. My Aunt Andi was getting married to my Uncle Stephen in my Grandmother's big house in Yonkers.

It was an imposing house from the outside with a formal driveway and lawn jockeys out front, and a wide terraced back yard full of fruit trees. Inside was homey, but also vast. I loved exploring it as a kid as it felt like the house the children in *The Lion, The Witch and the Wardrobe* were sent to stay in during the war. One visit I even tried pushing on the back of every closet wall, hoping to find an entrance to my own secret world.

Their wedding ceremony was in the living room, where I watched through the slats of the railing from the staircase landing. I mostly remember being jealous that my cousins Chris and Amanda got to participate in the actual ceremony. Never mind it was their mom getting married and they probably had rings to carry and flower petals to scatter.

In retrospect I was probably up there so I could see better. My memory of the service is mostly trying to see my aunt in her beautiful and flowing white dress next to my almost-uncle in tuxedo through the first row of adults standing with their backs to me.

Andi and Stephen would soon have a child, my cousin Peter, and their marriage was a happy and lasting one. And I was lucky to visit with them and my three cousins several times a year growing up.

It's fitting they got married in that house. It's where my Grammy Dickson and her husband Bill, your great-great grandfather, lived out their years together.

When they met back in the 1930s, he was booking talent for night clubs in New York. His claim to nightlife fame was being the first promoter on the East Coast to book a young Bob Hope.

They were both smart and had been good students, and coincidentally, both applied to and were accepted at Columbia University. But neither of them could afford to go. I like to think this bonded them to each other.

When they decided to get married, he took a job as a bank teller to have family-friendly hours. Flash forward a few decades, and he retired the president. I only knew him when I was very, very young so I can't remember him too well, but I imagine he was delightful, ambitious and a people person, like my grandmother.

They had three kids. My Dad was their oldest. I wasn't there for his wedding to my Mom, as I was a few years away from being around, but I have seen crisp black and white pictures. Let's take a look at them the next time we visit them in Maryland.

My Uncle Peter came next, and I attended his wedding as a kid. His fiancé worked for the Four Seasons, so their wedding and reception was in the ballroom of their Manhattan flagship hotel.

And my Aunt Andi was the youngest, whose second wedding is the one I just described.

We didn't go to a lot of other weddings growing up. Most of parent's friends were already married by the time I came along.

But as I became an adult, the generation of my cousins and my brother and I began to get married.

I was able to make it out to Rhode Island to see my cousin Chris marry his wife Lelei. It was a classy affair with a clambake rehearsal dinner and an outside tented reception on the water in Newport.

A funny highlight was the actor who has recently played Robin in the Batman movie series was in attendance. At first he acted super cool and stand-offish, I imagine expecting to be hounded by fans. But no one really noticed him, or if they did they didn't really care. So by the end of the night he was bumping into people on purpose on the dance floor and making a huge deal of apologizing, hoping we'd all acknowledge his celebrity.

But sadly, living so far away, I missed my cousin's Amanda's, Peter's, and Alexis' wedding. I wish I had been able to attend.

Some people despise weddings. And I can understand if they're anxious around lots of people or have been wronged in love.

But otherwise, what's not to like? There's good food, often an open bar, cake, dancing where no one cares if you can dance or not, and toasts. The toasts are my favorite part. Typically a parent stands up during the dinner and after the clinking of glasses dies down they share a story about the couple and some hopes for their shared future. Then maybe another parent or two gives a toast, and then a sibling or three and eventually best and good friends get up and say their piece.

Sometimes they are great stories about how they met, or what one of them was like when they were younger. Sometimes they are super touching and seem to be about the person giving them toast as much as the couple.

Those can make you tear up thinking about how amazing it is that two people can find each other and decide to spend the rest of their lives together.

And sometimes a toast goes completely off the rails. Those are the ones I tend to remember and relish the best. Inappropriate, rambling, completely off topic or all three. I've got a few favorites from weddings we attended. I won't share them here as they aren't really my stories to tell. But ask me about them sometime.

When your mom and I got married, we were lucky to have good toasts.

We were living in Los Angeles but had the ceremony up here in Portland. It's where we met, where our friends and our hearts were. We'd be moving back just a year later.

Surprising to neither of you I'm sure, your mom did most of the planning and work. And she did a great job.

We got married at the Museum of Contemporary Craft, which was just what it sounds like it was. A museum for artists working with textiles, clay and so on. They moved the current exhibition to the edges of the room and we had our ceremony and party right there in the main gallery.

It was quite the party. We had a good hundred and fifty people there, with friends and family from all over the country on hand. We didn't have a lot of money, so we had cupcakes instead of cake, and lots of appetizers instead of a seated dinner, but that just made it more fun and less formal. We did splurge on a storyteller slash babysitter so folks with kids could bring them but not have to mind them the whole time.

We also skipped any best man or bridesmaid business, and just walked together down the aisle to the Flaming Lips song "Do you Realize."

I can't remember as much of it as I like. I remember your mom looking stunning. And it is a little surreal to look out and see people from every part of my life looking up at us with delight. And like I said, the toasts were good. Some were even great. No one went off the rails, or at least not too far off. But after that honestly it went by in a kind of happy hazy blur.

Mostly I was just so overjoyed. Nervous, yes, but overjoyed we were doing this. Committing to being with each other, hoping to have kids (spoiler alert: we succeeded), and trying our best to make each other happy no matter what.

A sure sign that it was a good time was our friend Matt told us he never imagined getting married, but after coming to our wedding he could see himself going for it some day. Sure enough, he tied the knot some years later.

The first wedding the two of you attended was your Uncle Alex and Aunt Caitlyn's. They decided to get married July 4th in Washington DC close to where they and my parents live. And they asked me to be the officiant.

One visit to the Universal Life Church website later, and I was officially ordained and ready to help.

Washington DC was built on a swamp, so it's quite hot and humid in summer. The week of their wedding especially. It was a hundred and felt like a hundred and ten all week. And then the day of their wedding it started to pour. And it was an outside affair. Luckily just an hour before the ceremony the rain stopped, the clouds parted and the sun shone down.

Right on time.

The ceremony was wonderful. Alex and Caitlyn both looked fantastic and if they felt nervous they didn't show it. I had the same experience of seeing people from different parts of my life looking up at me with delight, being the officiant. But this time they were Alex's friends instead of mine.

And the reception aka the party was lots of fun. The whole affair was on a former estate turned event space, so it almost felt like a movie. The ceremony was poolside, there was a big tent where everyone ate and danced, and a grand house where the buffet and desserts were laid out and folks in the wedding could change.

Everett you were a bit of a handful, which is understandable considering you were only three. At the time you had this shock of curly blonde hair and mom put you in this cute sailor-themed dress shirt and pants. Which only made it all the more fun to see you jump into the fountain in the middle of the reception and to cool off and try and collect coins.

Pearl, after your flower girl duties were done, you spent a good part of the evening running around the grounds with all the other kids. You met Caitlyn's second and third cousins and were so happy to suddenly have a bigger family.

And while you never got to see all those second and third cousins of hers again, pretty soon you had your own new cousin, James. And more recently, Ellis came along. So your family, our family, continues to grow.

One day you guys might get married. If you do, here's some advice. Your job is not to make the other person happy, and especially not at the expense of yourself. But when you find the right person, making each other happy becomes contagious and starts to turn me or I into we. So here's my advice.

Really listen when they talk, and don't just hold onto the thing you want to say because when you're doing that you're not listening and by the time they are done talking what you wanted to share might not even be relevant anymore.

Figure out what brings them joy and give it to them. It doesn't have to be a trip to Paris. It can be as simple as remembering a fun little treat they love and surprising them with it the next time you go to the grocery store.

Pick up on their moods. If they need to process something, give them space to talk. If they need space, find something to do and don't invent reasons to suddenly interrupt them. And if they seem restless, come up with a wild idea and go have some fun.

And finally treat their success like your own success. Support them in achieving what they want to accomplish and celebrate it. Done right, you triple your wins. Because you'll have your own, theirs, and you'll both be more successful because you each have a real true partner helping you.

I guess that's really advice for any relationship, whether it's someone your date, someone you're family with or even just ways to keep a friendship strong.

Honestly, I don't have any preconceived ideas about either of you getting married or having a wedding. If you do, I think you'll both make great partners, but there's no pressure. At least not yet!

MUSIC

I've lived next door to a rock star not once but twice. They weren't capital "R" capital "S" rock stars, but they were rock stars.

The first was Nils Lofgren. He's a guitar player who played on some really big albums when he was young, including Neil Young's *After the Gold Rush*.

He lived next door to us when I was little. From our yard we could see him and his friends on his deck most nights, laughing and drinking beer.

I was just three or four, so I didn't care who he was. I was busy catching box turtles wandering through our yard and feeding them lettuce and carrots until my mom made me let them go.

At the time he was pursuing a critically renowned, but commercially unsuccessful, solo career. He moved away a year or two later to join Bruce Springsteen's E Street Band just in time to make the album *Born in the USA*. Good timing.

Bruce Springsteen was your Uncle Alex's favorite musician growing up. In fact I can't remember Alex liking or listening to anyone beside Bruce Springsteen. I wonder if Nils was partly the reason, or if that was just a coincidence.

My Uncle Peter gave my parents music every Christmas, which always made me a little jealous. I wanted music too! One year he gave them a then brand new "box set" that included several cassettes spanning Bruce Springsteen's career up to that point. It quickly became Alex's favorite possession.

When I was a kid I was more into my parents' record collection, the music from their younger days. They had albums by The Who, Neil Young, Jim Hendrix, Janis Joplin and several Beatles albums. The ones I really honed in on were the four they had from the later part of their career — *Rubber Soul, Revolver, Abbey Road and Sgt. Pepper's*.

Sgt. Pepper's was my favorite of the bunch. The cover alone was motivation for me to get my parents to show me how to take a record out of the sleeve without scratching it and memorize the sequence of levers and buttons to press to get the player to play.

Even though it was already well over a decade old, it felt entirely new to my ears. It introduced me to the idea of a concept album, but also the mind-blowing idea that these guys had invented another band to pretend they were in. What?

The Beatles were my favorite band for years on the strength of that album alone.

I didn't really listen to "contemporary" music until my friend Larry Kelly and I got into playing Dungeons and Dragons and realized the game was enhanced by a soundtrack. So we'd bring whatever new music we had discovered and share it with each other as we played.

At first we relied on the radio, which wasn't bad back then. You could hear singles from *Thriller, Born in the USA, She's So Unusual, Purple Rain* and *Synchronicity* in the same hour when I was eleven or twelve.

But we also wanted to hear stuff that wasn't for everyone. Music is a shared language that brings people together, but it can also be a secret knock that lets you into the door of a new subculture. We wanted in.

But it was hard, especially since we were in the 5th grade.

So we went to our local indie record store "Waxy Maxie" and worked up the courage to ask the clerk for "something cool." He looked at us, two kids who were decidedly not cool, and came back with a pair of tapes. One was an album from The Dead Kennedys, the other was The Dead Milkmen.

Maybe he had a sense of humor. Or maybe they were next to each other on the shelf.

I chose the Dead Kennedys tape and regretted it as soon as we listened to it. It was super fast with lots of treble, no bass, and the singing was very shrill. Even when I got into punk later on I could never get into the Dead Kennedys. The Dead Milkman were at least listenable.

So it was back to Top 40 and Classic rock for a few more years.

In high school I got introduced to the DC punk scene in high school by my friend Nick. That was pretty eye-opening. The musicians looked like audience members. And the music felt raw and immediate. Partly because you could go to a show and get to the front of the stage and be a few feet from the band, who was often only a little older than I was. And then buy a t-shirt directly from them right after they stopped playing.

I fell in love with local bands like Soul Side, Slant 6, and The Make-Up. But Fugazi was my favorite.

Do you know how a band or type of music can become a big part of your identity, at least for a little while? I think you do, Pearl. Everett, I'm not sure you can relate yet but I'm certain you will.

Listening to those bands made me want to start my own and made me think I could actually do it. Despite, as the cliche goes, not knowing how to play an instrument.

My attempts in high school failed when I asked for a guitar for Christmas and realized when I opened my big gift that I hadn't specified I wanted one that was electric.

When I went away to college at Wesleyan, I found myself surrounded by kids who loved the same music and were forming bands. I figured drums were the easiest path because there was no reading music involved. And it was all arms and legs, no fancy chords or finger positioning or trying to sing.

It took more rehearsing than I expected and a year of awkward auditions before I finally joined Dick Summer, ironically named by the three women who fronted the band after the 60s poet of the same name. My best friend Bill played bass so he and I formed the rhythm section as they all sang and played guitar and keyboard. I loved it.

When I moved to Portland after college, it was on. I saw live music five or six times a week and played in any band that would have me. In a few short years I saw hundreds of shows and played in a series of bands. A few were serious but the most fun ones had less a sense of purpose and more a sense of humor.

Manpower was a concept band with my friend Bill Tsitsos who sang and played bass. We both worked for the temp agency of the same name, so we would temp a different guitar player for each show who would learn all our songs and join us for just one show.

Mistress was also a concept band, imagined by my friend Justin. Were a send-up of 80s hair metal band playing for hip Portland crowds in on the joke. And we were pretty good. Most of the band worked for a big animation studio called Will Vinton staffed with folks new to town looking for fun on the weekends, and I was living in a massive warehouse space, so by our second show we were playing to hundreds of die-hard fans.

Our lead guitarist could finger tap metal solos and Justin was a fierce performer. He wrote a song called "High Horse" about a fictional ex who thought she was better than him. He would sing that song shirtless, running around the stage holding a toy hobby horse between his legs pretending to ride it, with his long hair swaying around.

I think Mistress could have gotten big, but Justin was pretty clear with us from the outset he was only starting the band to meet a girlfriend. And when he met a woman at our seventh show and started dating her, that was it. He quit the band and switched from band rehearsals to wedding planning.

Now that I think about it, around that time I did the same thing.

I met you mom in a very Portland 90s way. We had a mutual friend who worked for a developer, building some of the first lofts in an industrial part of town that would soon become the trendy Pearl District. Specifically it was on Everett Street, if that gives you some clues to where your names came from. Although Pearl, your name is also your great-great-grandmother's name on your mom's side.

The developer told our friend to get as many young people to come to the opening party on the promise of free food and an open bar to make the party feel young and hip, no matter none of us could have possibly afforded the lofts they were selling.

I met your mom in the model unit as we were both looking out the window at the city.

I was taken with her immediately. She had great style and was super fun but also smart, cute and very real. We hung out a few times getting to know each other, and then a few weeks after we met, she came to a show I was playing, and after the last song, she reached out to hold my hand and that was it. We didn't let go and haven't since.

From day one we were almost always listening to music.

Your mom used to play *The Who Sell Out* a lot. I loved the Who when I was younger but had never heard that album. Before the Internet you might know three of a band's albums really well, and have never even listened to the other four. Hearing that album still reminds me of our first few months together.

About a year after we met we decided to move in together to the apartment I was renting. That was the second time I lived next to a rock star. M. Ward lived across the hall. Although I think he might have still been Matt back then.

He was super nice. When we were living across from each other there was a big earthquake up in Washington, so strong it cracked the capital dome in Olympia and we could feel it here in Portland. It startled Susan, and she went out into the hallway wondering if she had imagined it, and saw Matt doing the same thing. He confirmed he felt it too.

Later on when he became successful, we listened to his album *Post-War* together quite a bit. The Magnetic Fields *69 Love Songs*, Arcade Fire *Funeral* and the Fucking Champs *III* were other albums we loved listening to together.

Those albums became the soundtracks to early years together when we were traveling back and forth between Portland and Los Angeles and flying to Europe to perform our eBay show together. I can hear a song off any of those albums and memories of our earlier life together come flooding back, like a time machine.

And then you two came along. Which has been amazing and at times challenging but also fun and beautiful.

Your collective presence in our life coincided with and maybe even caused the end of my playing and seeing live music. But it has meant, among many other awesome things, hearing the music you each discover and gaining new associations tied to your lives.

Pearl, whenever I hear the opening stanza of *Hard Knock Life* (from the Annie soundtrack but especially the Jay Z version) I can literally see you as a second grader with pigtails, stomping out on stage and announcing "Listen up orphans," in an Annie voice loud enough to reach the very back row of the room.

This was your very first theater camp, and your mom and I were excited for the production, and hoped you'd enjoy your performance. But wow. It was the moment we understood you had found a calling.

Hearing the band Ex-Hex's album *Rips* transports me to a field at Pickathon, and seeing something click as you immediately fell in love with their music. It was the first time you were drawn to music that Susan and I loved listening to too.

And my favorite nights of your tween years were when you heard us playing music from upstairs in your room, came down and asked to put on the next song. It usually leads to a game of rotating DJ with you and mom dancing together in the living room, or on either side of the kitchen from each other, dancing towards each other and crossing back and forth to the music.

Everett, I love that you've gone from asking for quiet during road trips to tolerating music to now requesting certain songs. And I appreciate how you treat music as a compliment to an activity.

The *Star Wars* soundtrack is great for playing Lego, especially Star Wars Lego. Sponge Bob Square Pants albums are for mouthing the lyrics, and when you're really feeling it, dancing along in the mirror. And there are several silly songs that make you find your sister and make her dance and play and run around the house with you because they make you nostalgic for your own shared memories together.

Most recently you have annexed the voice activated Apple speaker and we can often hear you through the vents asking Siri to play rock songs, pop anthems and the soundtrack music to your favorite video games.

I look forward to hearing the music you both fall in love with, and the music that becomes the soundtrack to your falling in love, and the songs that define the different parts and periods of your own life.

THANK YOU

Thanks to Kathy Hepinstall, B. Frayn Masters, Sara Guest, and Eric Meltzer for reading chapters early on and giving me notes and encouragement I needed to keep going. And to Aaron James for creating and collaboration on the cover and beyond.

Thanks to The Moth and the Portland Moth community for helping me understand the power of a great story and learn how to get better at telling them by hearing so many stories told by others.

And of course thanks to my family and friends for creating these stories with me. Mom, Dad, Alex, Caitlyn, James and Ellis, Grammy, Grandpa, Grammy, Grand Man, Peter, Andi, Dick, Charlie, Leslie, Lela, Stephen, Chris, Amanda, Peter, Erica, Ian, Stephen, Alexis, Michael, Jeanie, Julian, David and Dawn, and friends like Bill, Bill, Steve, Nick, Larry, Ryan, Betty Jo and David.

And most of all Pearl and Everett, and most most of all Susan.

Made in the USA
Middletown, DE
27 August 2023